Kids Behaving Badly

Teacher Strategies for Classroom Behaviour Problems

Emma Little

Copyright © Emma Little 2003
Pearson Education Australia
Unit 4, Level 2
14 Aquatic Drive
Frenchs Forest NSW 2086

www.pearsoned.com.au

The Copyright Act 1968 of Australia allows a maximum of one chapter or 10% of this book, whichever is the greater, to be copied by any educational institution for its educational purposes provided that that educational institution (or the body that administers it) has given a remuneration notice to Copyright Agency Limited (CAL) under the Act. For details of the CAL licence for educational institutions contact:
Copyright Agency Limited, telephone: (02) 9394 7600, email: info@copyright.com.au

All rights reserved. Except under the conditions described in the Copyright Act 1968 of Australia and subsequent amendments, no part of this publication may be reproduced, stored in a retrieval system or transmitted in any form or by any means, electronic, mechanical, photocopying, recording or otherwise, without the prior permission of the copyright owner.

Acquisitions Editor: Natalie Muir
Senior Project Editor: Julian Gray
Copy Editor: Janice Keynton
Cover design by Nada Backovic
Internal design by Dizign Pty Ltd
Typeset by Midland Typesetters, Maryborough, Vic.
Printed by Pearson Australia Demand Print Centre

1 2 3 4 5 07 06 05 04 03

National Library of Australia
Cataloguing-in-Publication Data

Little, Emma.
Kids behaving badly : teacher strategies for classroom behaviour problems.

Bibliography.
For teachers.
ISBN 1 74103 190 7.

1. Classroom management. 2. Parent-teacher relationships. 3. Behaviour modification. I. Title.

371.1024

Every effort has been made to trace and acknowledge copyright. However, should any infringement have occurred, the publishers tender their apologies and invite copyright owners to contact them.

An imprint of Pearson Education Australia

Contents

Preface	vi
Quick quiz	vii

Chapter 1 Introduction to behaviour problems — 1

Child centred effects	3
Effects on teachers	4
Effects on other children	5
Behaviour problems in the classroom: what are they?	6
Specific classroom behaviour problems	6
Classroom management: behavioural approach	9

Chapter 2 The effective teacher — 13

Withitness	14
Pace and predictability	15
Focus on positive behaviours and minimise reprimands	16
Clear expectations	16
Summary	18

Chapter 3 Establishing a positive environment — 19

Establishing class rules	20
Developing positive behaviours in your classroom	25

Chapter 4 Giving effective instructions and praise — 31

Giving effective instructions	32
Giving instructions to the whole class or small groups	33
Giving instructions to a child	34
Using praise in the classroom	35

Chapter 5 Consequences for problem behaviours — 39

Establishing logical consequences in the classroom	40
Time-out procedures for the classroom	42
Summary	46

Chapter 6 Specific behaviour problems— using the teacher tip sheets 47

1. Identify the problem 48
2. Implement the intervention 55
3. Plan for maintenance of appropriate behaviour 57
4. Do a follow up in three months 58
Summary 58

Teacher tip sheets

Talking out of turn 60
Hindering other children 62
Keeping on task 64
Poor social skills 66
Aggression 68
Withdrawn children 70
Disorganised children 72

Chapter 7 Parental involvement in behaviour management 75

Engage parents from the beginning of the year 77
Provide feedback for appropriate behaviour 77
Provide feedback for inappropriate behaviour 80
Parent/teacher conference 82

Chapter 8 Targeting specific groups 85

Attention Deficit Hyperactivity Disorder (ADHD) 86
Divorce and separation 92
Middle years of schooling 98

Chapter 9 Looking after yourself 105

Chapter 10 Final word 109

References 111

Appendix—Prize vouchers, token and certificate 116

Acknowledgements

I would like to thank Alan Hudson and Ray Wilks from RMIT University for their guidance, knowledge and support. I would particularly like to acknowledge their assistance in the development of the teacher tip sheets found later in this book. Thanks also goes to my parents, Ken and Lesley Wing Jan, for all their support. Finally, to Geoff for making me believe all things are possible!

Preface

Not too long ago I was speaking with a teacher about her experience teaching Year five students in a school known for having children who are fairly troublesome. I asked her what she did to manage the class. She said, 'Oh I have a good system. When they are naughty I get the children to stand with their nose against the chalkboard'. Trying to hide my horror, I asked her whether this works well. She responded, 'well sometimes it gets a bit crowded when there are seven or eight of them in a row'. She asked me if I had any suggestions, and this prompted me to start writing this book.

This book contains information for teachers about how to establish effective classroom management strategies. This is purposefully not a long and complex book as I know how busy teachers are, so this book contains ideas and strategies that really work. General management strategies are discussed with suggestions for implementation by classroom teachers. How to effectively work with parents is addressed as this is often an area that causes a great deal of teacher stress. Also included is a set of teacher tip sheets to assist teachers in dealing with specific behaviour problems. The tip sheets provide commonsense, effective strategies to deal with behaviour problems in primary school children.

I have created a 'Quick quiz' that will let you assess your own teaching behaviours and guide you to the parts of the book that will be most helpful for you. It is important to have good general classroom management strategies in place before you implement the teacher tip sheets to ensure that the suggested strategies have the best chance of being effective.

Quick quiz

	CIRCLE ONE RESPONSE		
1. I spend more time walking around the class than sitting at my desk.	TRUE	NOT TRUE	UNSURE
2. I can predict when a child is going to misbehave.	TRUE	NOT TRUE	UNSURE
3. I can stop misbehaviour before it gets out of control.	TRUE	NOT TRUE	UNSURE
4. I spend very little of my time dealing with behaviour problems.	TRUE	NOT TRUE	UNSURE
5. I feel in control in my classroom.	TRUE	NOT TRUE	UNSURE
6. I do not have children who behave poorly in my class.	TRUE	NOT TRUE	UNSURE
7. I am comfortable dealing with parents.	TRUE	NOT TRUE	UNSURE
8. I am not stressed.	TRUE	NOT TRUE	UNSURE
9. I have a positive relationship with my students.	TRUE	NOT TRUE	UNSURE
10. I have rules and consequences for inappropriate behaviours (that the children are aware of).	TRUE	NOT TRUE	UNSURE
11. I feel confident in parent/teacher interviews.	TRUE	NOT TRUE	UNSURE
12. I would like some new ideas for those troublesome behaviour problems.	TRUE	NOT TRUE	UNSURE
13. I would like to know more about how ADHD affects children.	TRUE	NOT TRUE	UNSURE
14. I would like to know what the effect of parental separation and divorce has on children and what I can do to help children adjust.	TRUE	NOT TRUE	UNSURE
15. I want to know how boys and girls differ in their classroom behaviours.	TRUE	NOT TRUE	UNSURE

If you answered NOT TRUE or UNSURE to any questions from 1–6, 9, or 10
The sections on the effective teacher, establishing a positive environment, giving instructions and praise and consequences will be most useful to start with.

If you answered NOT TRUE or UNSURE to question 7 or 11
The sections on parent/teacher conferences and involving parents in behaviour management strategies will be most useful to start with.

If you answered TRUE or UNSURE to question 12
The tip sheets will be the most useful to start with.

If you answered NOT TRUE or UNSURE to question 8
The section on looking after yourself is going to be most helpful to you.

If you answered TRUE of UNSURE to questions 13–15
The section on specific issues in the classroom will be most useful for you.

Introduction to children's behaviour problems

1

CHAPTER

Why should we worry about children's behaviour problems? Well apart from the stress they cause in the classroom, the number of children with challenging behaviours is increasing. Approximately 6% of school children have behaviour problems that would be considered so serious that they require specialist intervention (Little, Hudson & Wilks 2000). In addition to these 6% of children, there are many more children whose behaviour in the classroom significantly interferes with their own and other children's learning. Therefore, classroom teachers are likely to have children in their classrooms that cause significant disruption and require a substantial amount of teacher attention and behaviour management.

Child misbehaviour in the classroom results in decreased opportunities to learn for the individual child and his peers. A child with behaviour problems is likely to have social difficulties with peers, and this is exacerbated when combined with the tendency for children with behaviour problems to be highly impulsive with a negative attitude (Pullis 1991). In addition to the child centred effects, behaviour problems in students can also cause high levels of work related stress and personal distress in teachers (Miller 1995). Problem behaviours have been found to divert the teacher's attention from instructing the class and cause excess time to be spent engaged in disciplinary action (Lochman, Lampron, Gemmer & Harris 1987). When teachers were asked if they spent more time on problems of order and control than they should, 51% of teachers said yes. The other, often neglected, group to suffer the effects of a child with behaviour problems in the classroom is the rest of the class (Short & Shapiro 1993).

Behaviour problems in children are a significant risk factor for the development of later antisocial adult behaviour (Fergusson, Horwood & Lynskey 1994; Kazdin 1995). Therefore, it is important to identify children with behaviour problems at an early age and intervene before these behaviours are no longer under the control of the child's parents or teachers. It is especially important to deal with these behaviours in the primary school years, as the amount of time a single teacher spends with the child is far greater than in secondary school. Therefore you as a teacher can have a significant impact on the child because you can make sure that there are consistent expectations in the classroom.

While there is no doubt that the home environment is most likely the principal setting where children's behaviour problems need to be addressed, for one reason or another often this intervention does not occur. Once children reach primary school, the classroom becomes of prime importance for intervention as this is the setting in which children spend the majority of their time away from home. When a child demonstrates behaviour

CHAPTER 1 ▓ INTRODUCTION TO CHILDREN'S BEHAVIOUR PROBLEMS

problems in both the home and school setting this has serious implications for management. If intervention targets only one setting for the conduct disordered child, the disruptive and problem behaviours may occur in the other setting/s resulting in the behaviours persisting through to deviancy in adolescence. The need for classroom management of conduct problems addressing multiple settings are emphasised in the research (Dodge 1993). The important finding from the research is that even if you can not get parents to make changes at home, making changes in the classroom will make a difference. Children will learn that what they do at home will not be accepted at school.

Children with behaviour problems cause a great deal of concern for teachers and parents alike. They may have tried many different ways of managing these children with little success. While it is often hoped for, children with serious behaviour problems generally do not grow out of their 'naughty' behaviour. In fact, if these problems are not adequately managed these children may go on to displaying even more serious and problematic behaviours. Therefore, it is important that teachers identify these behaviours and intervene early. Sometimes teachers may find that they have to put a lot of energy into managing behaviour problems and this takes their time away from teaching. This can be exacerbated if teachers do not have access to effective strategies for dealing with these problem behaviours. In fact, a number of researchers have found that teachers do not believe that their initial training provided them with all the skills necessary to manage classroom and behaviour problems (Merrett & Wheldall 1993; Giallo & Little 2003). Both in research and in speaking with teachers it is clear that classroom and behaviour management are areas that they believe are vitally important to teaching.

There are many reasons why teachers should actively work on minimising misbehaviour in the classroom. Teachers need to be in control of their class's behaviour as child misbehaviour results in decreased opportunities to learn for the individual child and his peers. A child with behavioural and or social problems is likely to have relationship difficulties with peers as well as academic difficulties. The impact on the child, the teacher, and the rest of the class can not be understated.

Child centred effects

Behaviour problems have been found to be related to a number of academic and social problems. For example, children with behaviour problems often have lowered academic motivation and performance, and poorer social skills than their peers (Pullis 1991; Short &

Shapiro 1993). Therefore, students who have high levels of disruptive behaviour may demonstrate problems with staying on task, not calling out, being organised and interacting appropriately with their peers.

These difficulties in task related behaviours and decreased academic performance can then lead to the child falling behind the class and not understanding the academic content of class activities. The child may then become bored, lack attention from the teacher, and become disruptive in order to gain attention and to combat the boredom. This creates a cycle of difficult behaviour and poor academic progress that becomes increasingly severe unless intervention is initiated.

Academic difficulties and failure have been identified as significant risk factors for adolescent delinquency and problems in the middle years of schooling (Loeber 1990). When there is intervention to address the child's behaviour in the classroom, the child can spend more time engaged in academic activities and less time behaving inappropriately. Often children who act out in the classroom are doing so because they get something out of it. Their behaviour may gain them attention from the teacher or the rest of the class (remember for some children, any attention is better than none). Alternatively, their behaviour may allow them to divert attention away from difficulties with academic tasks, and may allow them to avoid working altogether. Finally, they may behave the way they do because they do not know, or do not have the skills, to behave in a more appropriate way.

Effects on teachers

I probably do not need to tell you the effect of behaviour problems on the teacher—if you are reading this then you probably have experienced it first hand. However, there is a lot of research that shows the common effects of child behaviour problems on teachers.

Behaviour problems in students can cause high levels of work related stress in teachers. If a teacher does not believe that he/she can control these behaviour problems, then his/her sense of success as a teacher may be affected. It can start to feel like the children are in control and not the teacher. Not knowing effective management strategies can lead to teachers trying lots of different ways to handle the child with behaviour problems and the teacher might find that he/she frequently is unsuccessful in dealing with the child. Given the variety of philosophies towards classroom management, teachers can start to feel

CHAPTER 1 ■ INTRODUCTION TO CHILDREN'S BEHAVIOUR PROBLEMS

pulled in many directions. So in this book I am going to provide you with strategies that work!

If you are looking for effective strategies then you will find them here. It is important that as a teacher you have a repertoire of strategies that work because behaviour problems in the classroom can cause personal distress in teachers and lead to stress and sometimes burnout. If you are feeling stressed, later on in this book I am going to give you some ideas on how to take care of yourself (teachers tend to look after everyone else first).

In my many discussions with teachers, there seems to be a general theme that they do not feel they were well prepared to deal with classroom management issues. Research has also found that teachers do not report that their initial training provided them with the skills necessary to manage classroom and behaviour problems (Giallo & Little 2003; Little 1999; Merrett & Wheldall 1993). Both recent graduate teachers and more experienced teachers find managing classroom behaviour problems is a major cause of stress. It is often the case that teachers are not aware of effective ways to quickly deal with behaviour problems, and end up spending a lot of time and energy trying to maintain control. With all the other tasks that a teacher must undertake, strategies for classroom management need to be simple and straightforward to implement.

Effects on other children

Other children in the classroom are also greatly affected by the behaviour of individual children. Behaviour problems have been found to divert the teacher's attention from instructing the class, resulting in the teachers spending more time engaged in disciplinary action than should be necessary (Giallo & Little 2003; Lochman, Lampron, Gemmer & Harris 1987). Having a child with behaviour problems in the classroom (whose behaviour is not being managed) can result in decreased learning time for the whole class. Also, children sitting with a child who is off task may be distracted. The whole classroom atmosphere can become tense and teacher attention is often focused on the disruptive child rather than on the rest of the class.

Behaviour problems in the classroom setting quite clearly have widespread effects on the child, the teacher, and the rest of the class. Therefore, teachers need to have strategies that they can use to manage these behaviours. There are many different theories about how children's behaviour problems should be managed. This book is not designed to provide

5

you with a review of all the theoretical approaches to classroom management, there are many good texts on this subject already. Rather, my aim is to give you strategies that have been shown to work, and these strategies are based on the behavioural approach.

Behaviour problems in the classroom: what are they?

It is commonly thought that the behaviours that teachers are most concerned about are serious infringements of rules and violations of the rights of others. A great deal of media attention is given to violence in schools, use of weapons, gang activities and vandalism. As a result, we can start to think that if we only have children who are doing frequent minor irritating behaviours in the classroom then we are doing well. I am not undermining the seriousness of these more violent and aggressive behaviours and the need for assistance in dealing with students who engage in them. However, these are not the behaviours that teachers are most concerned about and are not the behaviours that are the cause of teacher stress and burnout. Rather, the more serious behaviours occur relatively infrequently and do not generally cause regular disruption to the day-to-day running of a classroom. Those minor but frequent irritants are the ones that cause the most stress and disruption and are also the early signs of behaviour problems that could lead to the more serious antisocial acts.

Specific classroom behaviour problems

Surveys of teachers have demonstrated that there are specific classroom behaviour problems that teachers frequently have to deal with in their day-to-day running of the classroom (Little 2001; Wheldall & Merrett 1988). Teachers frequently report spending too much time on these issues of order and control. In addition, many teachers do not believe they have enough information, support and training to effectively manage these behaviour problems.

The most troublesome behavioural problems reported by both primary school teachers and secondary school teachers are 'talking out of turn' and 'hindering other children' (Little 2001; Wheldall & Merrett 1988)—the TOOTs and the HOCs. Talking out of turn involves calling out during times when the teacher or other children are speaking. It also involves

CHAPTER 1 ■ INTRODUCTION TO CHILDREN'S BEHAVIOUR PROBLEMS

children not putting their hands up and waiting for their turn to speak when engaging in class discussions. This results in the teacher constantly having to ask children to wait their turn, and can disrupt the flow of classroom discussions. Calling out can also result in the more compliant and quieter children missing out on the opportunity to contribute to class discussions. It also interferes with other children's ability to think about issues and come to their own conclusions.

Hindering other children is typically the second most troublesome behaviour found in the primary school setting. Hindering other children involves a whole range of distractive behaviours that result in other children (who would normally be on task) being disrupted and spending less time on their school work. Behaviours such as talking instead of working, engaging in 'clowning around' to gain the attention of other children, and generally drawing other children away from their own work can be very disruptive to the entire class.

The other behaviours that were also identified by these researchers as being troublesome included:

- **Disobedience**—generally not doing as the teacher has asked. This can be direct defiance, or more subtle forms of disobedience such as only doing part of what was requested.

- **Idleness/slowness**—children who work slowly. This does not include students who do not have the ability to complete the work. Rather, children who spend a large amount of time being idle or work exceedingly slowly for no apparent reason.

- **Making unnecessary noise**—teachers frequently report unnecessary noise as being a cause of disruption in the classroom. This can take many forms from exceedingly loud voices through to noise made by banging on tables.

- **Aggression**—this includes both verbal and physical aggression. It is not uncommon for some children to hit out at their peers. Kicking, hitting, biting, pinching and so on are seen in some school children.

Anecdotally, teachers have also reported that they are concerned about:

- **Children's organisational skills**—having to constantly remind children about having the right books and equipment can be extremely frustrating. Some children seem to find it a real challenge to keep their books, desks, and bags tidy and often seem to be oblivious to the routines of the classroom. Constantly reminding children about what books to get out and to bring back notices and so on can cause a great deal of stress for the teacher.

- **Social behaviours**—children who have difficulty interacting with other children and in the classroom environment can cause a great deal of concern for both parents and teachers. Some children will hardly ever, if at all, volunteer a response in the classroom and may appear quite withdrawn.

- **Staying on task**—this involves those children who have to be constantly monitored to ensure they are doing what is expected. These children may move from task to task and may use a variety of diversionary tactics to ensure that they do not persist at the required work.

All of these behaviour problems may initially start as quite minor in severity, however they can interfere with the teacher's ability to teach and manage the classroom. In addition, intervening with these specific behaviour problems may prevent the child going on to develop more serious behavioural problems.

Addressing these behaviours early on in the child's years at school may prevent later escalation of behaviour problems. These behaviours alone are easily manageable in the classroom setting and reducing these difficulties will not only impact on the child's behaviour but also on the general classroom environment. Often teachers will find that they have a number of children in their classrooms demonstrating one or more of these problem behaviours. Teachers can begin to feel stretched in all directions and unsure as to how to manage each child.

The tip sheets that are presented later in this book cover seven of the most commonly occurring classroom behaviour problems, as reported by teachers:

(1) talking out of turn,

(2) hindering other children,

CHAPTER 1 ▓ INTRODUCTION TO CHILDREN'S BEHAVIOUR PROBLEMS

(3) poor social skills,

(4) withdrawn children,

(5) aggression,

(6) disorganised children, and

(7) keeping on task.

The tip sheets provide specific strategies for dealing with each of these problems and have been demonstrated to be effective in modifying the behaviour of primary school children (Little, Hudson & Wilks 2002). The advice presented in the teacher tip sheets is based on established theories of applied behaviour analysis (which will be discussed below) and have been demonstrated to be effective. These tip sheets were developed and tested in consultation with teachers in Victorian schools.

When I first began working on the tip sheets, I spent a lot of time talking with teachers about what they needed to know in order to deal with behaviour problems. Teachers generally said that they needed more specific ideas on what to do with a common set of behaviour problems. Many of the strategies we came up with are not new, are not particularly innovative, but are put together from suggestions made by teachers. They are also put together in such a way that they provide step-by-step instructions and ideas on managing the behaviour problems.

Classroom management: behavioural approach

The strategies discussed in this book take a behavioural approach to classroom management. Canter's *Assertive discipline* (1976, 1982) should be acknowledged as a seminal work in this area, and the strategies suggested in this text have a lot of similarity to Canter's application of behavioural principles in the classroom. Such an approach assumes that misbehaviour is maintained by conditions in the environment (Tingstrom & Edwards, 1989). The teacher can use specific strategies to manage misbehaviour, regardless of whether the initial cause of behaviour problems is due to the home environment, internal factors (e.g. ADHD, illness, poor self-control), or previous experiences in the classroom.

This type of approach does not require the teacher having information about where or why the behaviour initially started; rather, what is happening now to keep that behaviour going.

The teacher needs to be aware of the triggers of a student's behaviour and can then work to alter the environment so that appropriate behaviour is more likely to occur than inappropriate behaviour. It is important to understand that such an approach does not imply that the behaviour is the result of something that the teacher has done. Rather, it accepts that often the causes of behaviour problems can not be identified or directly addressed. Regardless of the cause, there are ways to change the environment to reduce the likelihood of behaviours occurring. Therefore, even if a child's behaviour is a problem at home, just by changing the way the behaviour is dealt with in the classroom can result in significant improvements. This is very encouraging for teachers who are unable to get parental assistance to manage their child's behaviour.

The basic assumption behind this model is that not all children instinctively 'know' how to be well-behaved in the classroom, but need to be taught to develop the appropriate behaviours. Using strategies such as reinforcement to increase more acceptable behaviours is viewed as an effective method of behaviour management that also enhances children's self-esteem. As part of this type of approach, children are involved in the setting of class rules early on in the year and in the setting of effective consequences for inappropriate behaviour. Such a model is positively oriented, provides a structured learning setting and focuses on the children's appropriate behaviours instead of giving attention for inappropriate behaviours (Gordon, Arthur & Butterfield 1996; Wolfgang & Glickman 1980). Therefore, the child learns what to do, rather than just what not to do, and teaches them important life skills (such as managing their emotions, respecting others, and that there are consequences for all our behaviour).

A behavioural approach to classroom behaviour management incorporates a number of the elements of effective teaching. The teacher and class establish class rules and consequences and the teacher ensures the students know what is expected. The focus of such an approach is on positive interactions and skill building to develop appropriate behaviours. As the positive elements are easy to administer, there need not be disruptions to the teaching session. Lessons can be rapid-paced and overlapping, both of which are characteristics of effective teaching. Teachers who use such an approach are focused on the class as a whole and do not spend extended periods of lesson time devoted to

CHAPTER 1 ▓ INTRODUCTION TO CHILDREN'S BEHAVIOUR PROBLEMS

reprimanding one child. Therefore the teacher is able to monitor all children and can be said to have 'withitness' (as first described by Kounin in 1970). Therefore, the behavioural model has much support as being an effective and efficient way to manage children's classroom behaviours.

Both the classroom management strategies recommended in this book and the tip sheets for specific behaviour problems are based on this behavioural approach to classroom management. Before the procedures involved with the tip sheets are introduced, some general classroom management strategies will be discussed. It is important that we have a solid understanding of what makes effective teachers. The 'Quick quiz' at the start of the book (page vii) will let you assess your own teaching behaviours and guide you to the parts of the book that will be most helpful for you. It is important to have good general classroom management strategies in place before you implement the teacher tip sheets to ensure that the suggested strategies have the best chance of being effective.

The effective teacher

CHAPTER 2

Students' learning does not solely depend on the material presented to them by their teacher, in fact this is not even the most important aspect of teaching. In order for this knowledge to be imparted effectively the teacher must have a number of other skills apart from the instructional procedures. One of the most vital skills an effective teacher needs is that of classroom management. If children are not listening to and concentrating on the information presented, there is little likelihood of this information being stored.

Early definitions of teacher effectiveness defined it as the amount of progress the students make toward a specific educational goal (Bell & Davidson 1976). Therefore, the result of effective teaching is to bring about the desired level of student learning from some educational activity. Teachers' managerial skills, behaviour management and instructional procedures have a direct effect on how much of their students' time is spent on task. This academic learning time in turn influences student achievement level (Brophy 1982).

Classrooms are filled with students, all with different abilities, interests, personalities and goals who must share resources, modify their behaviour on demand, and participate in many different tasks (Woolfolk 1993). Teachers are finding that their roles are continually expanding and they have more and more tasks to take care of (Elson-Green 2002). When managing a classroom, teachers are required to maximise student involvement in learning activities, minimise disruptions and make efficient use of instruction time (Emmer, Evertson & Anderson 1980). Jerome Freiberg (1983) wrote 'classroom management is an important dimension of teaching because management activities lead to the establishment and maintenance of those conditions in which instruction can take place effectively and efficiently' (p. 1). So how do effective teachers manage a classroom in order to prevent behaviour problems? A number of teacher characteristics are associated with teacher effectiveness and we will now look at these in turn.

Withitness

One characteristic of effective teachers is 'withitness' (Kounin 1970). While this is a relatively old concept, it is still a vital ingredient in the effective classroom. Teachers who demonstrate to the children that they have 'eyes in the back of their head' and know what they are doing at any one point, are said to have 'withitness'.

To demonstrate 'withitness' teachers need to be monitoring their class at all times. This might involve walking around the classroom when children are engaged in independent

CHAPTER 2 ■ THE EFFECTIVE TEACHER

work and being 'near the action'. If you are sitting at your desk for extended periods of time then there is a chance that you are not seeing all that the children are doing.

Other ways that teachers can demonstrate 'withitness' include placing the student desks so the teacher can have visual eye contact with all students. This is often not popular in classrooms as there is a trend for tables to be structured in more social group arrangements. I should emphasise that this is fine for children who are able to regulate their own behaviour and focus on their own work when required. However, for those children who are easily distracted or likely to distract other children, this type of set up can be a source of temptation. At the very least these children should be seated so that they are close to where you give instructions (and can keep an eye on them) and are away from as many distractions as possible.

Apart from minimising time spent at the teacher's desk and seating children so that you can have eye contact, another element of withitness is close monitoring. This involves keeping a close eye on children who have a tendency to become distracted or disruptive. This is done by keeping on the move in the classroom so you are often physically near the child and keeping a regular visual check on what the child is doing. The benefit of this monitoring is that it can lead to a reduced need to manage disciplinary problems, because the teacher can quickly identify an inappropriate behaviour before it becomes a problem.

Pace and predictability

Effective teachers keep the class moving and let the children know in advance what is coming up (Good & Brophy 1994). One easy way to do this is to have a weekly schedule that is visible to all children, like the one below. This timetable can be changed each week and should be easy for students to see and understand.

WHAT WE ARE DOING THIS WEEK					
	MONDAY	**TUESDAY**	**WEDNESDAY**	**THURSDAY**	**FRIDAY**
MORNING	LITERACY	LITERACY	LITERACY	LITERACY	LITERACY
RECESS					
MIDMORNING	MATHS	MATHS	MATHS	MATHS	MATHS
	ITALIAN	SOSE	SPORT	LIBRARY	SCIENCE
LUNCH					
AFTERNOON	ART	READING	EXCURSION	HEALTH	SPORT

Lessons should overlap so that there is plenty of opportunity for revising information and building on past knowledge. There are plenty of useful texts on the mechanics of teaching each area of the curriculum, so this will not be addressed here.

The transition between lessons should also be smooth. This means making sure you have all the equipment you need before you begin the day. Having a box or folder devoted to each area of the curriculum can be handy as all you have to do is grab that before you begin. The more time you have in between lessons, the more opportunity students have to start misbehaving and to lose their academic focus. In an effective teacher's classroom more time is devoted to academic activities with classes organised in one large group. Children know what to expect in each lesson and the teacher is organised so that there is little time spent between lessons working out what he/she has to do next.

Some practical ways to improve pace and predictability include:

- having an established 'teaching' area where you have a whiteboard (or chalkboard), textas, rulers, frequently used books and so forth. Children know that when they are sitting in front of that area they are learning something important.

CHAPTER 2 ▨ THE EFFECTIVE TEACHER

- having a timetable or task board on a poster in your classroom so that children know what is happening across the day and across the week. You can use a laminated blank timetable and use an erasable whiteboard marker to fill in each day's activities.

- spending 30 minutes each morning (before students arrive) laying out all the materials you will need for the day's lessons to ensure that you can move quickly and smoothly from one activity to another.

- sticking to a fairly consistent routine so that children who are disorganised, or who do not cope well with change are not having to try to deal with adapting to constantly changing programs.

Focus on positive behaviours and minimise reprimands

Effective teachers use more praise and positive motivation than ineffective teachers (Sutherland 2000). Effective teachers do not interrupt the lesson by delivering drawn out reprimands or overreactions to student misbehaviour (Brophy 1982). Rather, effective teachers need only cue attention with a brief comment and focus on praise rather than threatening punishment. Later in this book we will look at ways of establishing effective behaviour management strategies.

Clear expectations

Another characteristic of effective teachers is the involvement of students in establishing appropriate behaviours and inappropriate behaviours in the initial phase of the school year (Wilson & Wing Jan 1995). The effective teacher spends time teaching and re-enforcing classroom rules during the first few weeks. Rules are displayed and when a student behaves inappropriately they are referred to the rules and reminded of the agreed behaviours (Wilson & Wing Jan 1995). In the next chapter we will go through the process of setting up classroom rules.

17

Summary

In summary, it is evident that effective teachers have characteristics and behaviours which are not found in the ineffective teacher's repertoire of skills. These include 'withitness', rule setting, reinforcement, rapid pacing, lesson overlap and more time engaged in academic activities. What follows is a description of establishing a positive learning environment as part of the classroom behaviour management strategy.

Establishing a positive environment

CHAPTER 3

As already mentioned, there are specific, effective strategies that teachers can use in their classrooms to increase the use of appropriate behaviours and decrease the frequency of inappropriate behaviours by children. These include establishing class rules, focusing on positive behaviours, giving clear instructions, and using appropriate consequences. A whole-school approach to classroom management should include these elements to ensure that all children know that every teacher has the same expectations and the same procedure for dealing with behaviour. However, if your school does not have a consistent approach to classroom management then you might need to set up your own program within your classroom. This will work effectively for the students in your class, however you may need to go through the process at the beginning of each year as the new students may not have experienced a similar approach in past classrooms.

This section provides practical suggestions on how to set up effective strategies in your classroom. We will look at overall classroom management and specific teacher behaviours. It is important to remember that these procedures should be in place before you use the specific tip sheet strategies, as generally the idea of the overall classroom management strategies is to set up an environment that prevents problems as much as possible. If you do not have adequate levels of classroom control to begin with then the tip sheet strategies are going to be less than optimally effective.

It should be emphasised that how you approach behaviour management in your classroom must be consistent with the state welfare and school policies that govern your classroom. It is also a good idea to liaise with your team leader or principal so that your direct supervisors are aware of your procedures and are supportive. This is particularly important for procedures such as letters home, time out and logical consequences as some schools and/or states may have restrictions regarding their use.

Establishing class rules

At the beginning of the school year it is important to explicitly state the expectations you have in your classroom and the behaviour that you expect from the children. One very effective method of doing this is to establish a set of class rules. These rules need to be ones that are important for the smooth running of the classroom and for the development of respect within the class.

CHAPTER 3 ▩ ESTABLISHING A POSITIVE ENVIRONMENT

Involving children in the creation of classroom rules and consequences is an effective way of making the rules important and meaningful to the children. Allowing children the opportunity to negotiate the rules ensures that the class understands the reasons for each rule and it allows the children to have input into how they want their class to function. Children are likely to stick to rules that they believe are important. However, it is also important that *you* get the final say on the rules so that you are setting yourself up as the leader in the classroom.

Setting up rules is one of the tasks you can do on the very first day of school. It demonstrates to the children that there is an atmosphere of mutual respect in the classroom and that there are clear boundaries for their behaviour. Children respond well to rules when they are reasonable, clear and developed in a cooperative atmosphere (provides a feeling of ownership and group cohesiveness).

Steps in establishing rules

1. Set aside a session in the first week of school (preferably in the first day) that you will devote to establishing class rules through class negotiation.

2. Explain to the children that class rules will ensure that there are certain behaviours that are expected in the classroom and that these behaviours are ones that will help make the class a happy and supportive one. Generally these rules will be associated with safety or courtesy.

3. Brainstorm a list of behaviours that the children think are needed for a classroom to run smoothly (include any ideas to start off with—even the silly ones). If the children do not think of ones that you consider important, then you can suggest these to them as well.

4. Once you have a large list of ideas, ask the children to pick five or six of the most important rules. You can get them to put into their own words why they are important. This could even be a written activity. These will then form your class rules.

5. The list should be framed in the positive—i.e. instead of 'don't call out' use 'put your hand up and wait to be asked to speak'. When they are phrased positively it teaches

21

children what to do (rather than simply what not to do) and creates a more friendly atmosphere. A whole list of 'don'ts' can make the classroom feel quite dictatorial.

6. Have the children role play each of the rules (particularly useful for younger grade levels). Ask different children to demonstrate what it means to follow the rules (i.e. putting their hands up to answer questions). This ensures that all children know exactly what it is that they must do. It also makes learning the rules more interesting and fun than you telling them what they have to do.

7. Discuss with the children some of the possible consequences of breaking each rule. You can involve them in generating a list of consequences if you like. The consequences need to be appropriate to the rule for them to be most effective. For example if a child says something nasty to another child then he/she must write a letter of apology. Some examples of consequences are included below.

RULE	CONSEQUENCE IF YOU DON'T FOLLOW THE RULE
1. Put your hand up to speak	Practise putting up your hand
2. Bring your homework to school	Doing a homework sheet at lunchtime
3. Look after others' property	Replacing property you lose or ruin
4. Walk in the classroom	Practise walking slowly

8. Display the class rules in a prominent position in the classroom. This is extremely important as many children need visual and verbal reminders of the rules. At the end of this section is an example of a poster for class rules that you could enlarge and display in your own classroom. The rules could also be typed up as individual sheets for children to take home or put in their diary.

9. Periodically go through the class rules with the children to make sure that they remember the rules and consequences and understand that these are important and valued.

CHAPTER 3 ■ ESTABLISHING A POSITIVE ENVIRONMENT

Example of class rules

IN OUR CLASS WE:
1. Put our hand up and wait to be asked to speak.
2. Listen carefully when someone else is speaking.
3. Take care of other people's belongings.
4. Speak in a talking voice when in the classroom.
5. Only say nice things to other people in our class.

10. Finally and most importantly, praise children who follow the rules. Take every opportunity to point out when someone is doing the right thing. This serves two purposes: (1) doing the right thing gets recognised and (2) it provides the other children with peer models.

Classroom rules set the tone of your classroom and invite the children to respect each other and the process of learning. They also ensure that children recognise that there are boundaries in the classroom regarding behaviour and sets you up as the leader of the classroom, which allows you to get on with the job of teaching. On the next page I have provided you with a sample rules sheet that you could enlarge and complete for your class.

KIDS BEHAVING BADLY

IN OUR CLASS WE:

1. _____

2. _____

3. _____

4. _____

5. _____

CHAPTER 3 ▦ ESTABLISHING A POSITIVE ENVIRONMENT

Developing positive behaviours in your classroom

A positive classroom environment may be created using rewards for appropriate behaviour. This can be done through the use of certificates, tangible rewards (stickers, stamps, etc.) or access to desired activities. Involving the whole class in working towards a reward for appropriate behaviour can increase their sense of unity and create a feeling of belonging. This chapter deals with setting up a structured reward system in your classroom to promote positive behaviours.

Setting up such a system in your classroom will complement your rule system and will ensure that all children get the opportunity to be rewarded for 'doing the right thing'.

Once you have classroom rules, you may want to use a strategy in your classroom that rewards children for following the rules. Such a strategy sets up a 'game' in your classroom where the object is to earn points/tokens for appropriate behaviour. These points/tokens that each child earns are added to a central collection for the whole class or for a smaller team within the class and once a specific number is reached there is some bigger reward. There are a number of formal programs to develop a positive classroom environment. One that has worked successfully in many Australian schools is the 'Fly Me To the Moon' program developed by Cullen and Wilks (1983). This program provides teachers with step-by-step strategies to establish positive classroom behaviours.

The basic process in setting up a positive behaviour program in your classroom is outlined below and is based on the model developed by Cullen and Wilks (1983). Remember, while it may take some planning initially, very quickly the effort you have to put in to see positive behaviours will reduce. Children will want to do the right thing because they see the benefit in doing so. It also helps to create a cooperative atmosphere within your classroom.

1. Decide whether you want the whole class to work together, or smaller teams within the class. Sometimes the element of competition between groups is an additional motivator. However, if you want to create a really cohesive classroom, then it is best to start with the whole class working together.

    If you use small groups, make sure you mix children up so they are not with their friends, and so there is a good spread of abilities within each group. These two

25

elements are crucial to encourage friendships across the class, and gives each group an equal chance of 'winning'.

2. Decide what it is that the children will work towards. Weekly prizes work well.

   For teams within the class:

   ▨ At the end of the week the team with the most points gets:

   – a certificate, sticker or voucher (see Appendix for some examples to use)

   – a desired position of responsibility

   – to choose a game/activity to do in the last session.

   For the whole class, the class gets:

   – a favourite activity in the last session on Friday.

   – points towards an end of term excursion/event (e.g. each week the class can earn up to 50 points and if they have 400 points by the end of term they can have a party, special lunch etc.)

   – certificates, stickers or vouchers (see Appendix for some ideas and examples to use)

   – anything else you can think of.

3. Once you have decided on how many groups you will have (i.e. teams or class) and what the class will work towards, then you need to do the following:

   ▨ **Sell the plan to the class.**
   You can describe it as a game where the goal is to earn enough points to get to do something really special. They need to be motivated to earn the reward. Create a poster, or special picture on the board where they can see how many points they have earned (see the example opposite). You could also use a glass jar with lines on the side and coloured counters that are placed in the jar.

CHAPTER 3 ■ ESTABLISHING A POSITIVE ENVIRONMENT

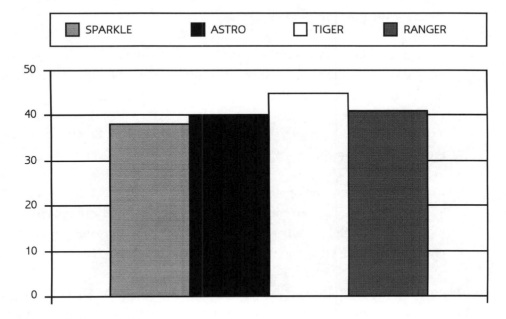

- Discuss the behaviours that will earn them points (these could be your class rules). Perhaps pick a couple of behaviours that are problematic in your classroom as well as one that is not so much of a problem.

  - To start off with you may just want to focus on one behaviour, then add more as the children get used to this system.

- If working with teams then you should select the teams ensuring that there are a variety of abilities in each group. Children can give their team a name to create a sense of ownership and unity.

- Set up the point collection system. Are you going to tally them on the board? Put tokens in a container? Add paperclips to a paperclip chain? Younger children typically respond better to more visual strategies like tokens.

- Explain that you will be monitoring the class and when you see someone following the rules you will give their team (or the class) a point (or whatever you have decided they will earn).

- It is a good idea to try to catch the children who often misbehave doing the right thing and not just the ones that do the right thing most of the time (of course they need to be rewarded as well).

- At the end of the week tally up the points and make sure that the children receive the promised reward.

- At the start of each week you can change the behaviour that earns the rewards. This ensures that you are constantly developing new skills in the children, and provides continued novelty so that children remain interested. You can also change the reward that you use.

This sort of strategy in the classroom allows you to reduce the amount of time you have to spend reminding children about how to behave. Children love trying to 'earn' the tokens and as a result are very aware of monitoring their own behaviour. It takes very little time for you to deliver the points/tokens and if you create a bright, attractive poster it provides a constant reminder of what is expected and how the

CHAPTER 3 ▪ ESTABLISHING A POSITIVE ENVIRONMENT

children are going in working towards their goal. This nicely complements the rules that you have established for your classroom and helps to create an environment where cooperation and respect for others are valued.

30

Giving effective instructions and praise

CHAPTER 4

Another important area of classroom management is developing the skills for giving instructions to students. In order for you to communicate the expectations you have for the classroom you need to have good, clear strategies for instruction giving. Many children with behaviour problems, attentional difficulties or short-term auditory memory problems will have difficulty in listening to and understanding instructions if they are not communicated in a very specific way. In this section, I give you some ideas for delivering instructions that are likely to be listened to and followed by all children, even the most inattentive of students.

Giving effective instructions

It is easy to fall into the trap of giving instructions or directions to children that are vague, incomplete or difficult for the child to follow. If your instructions are not specific then you run the risk of:

- children not understanding them (which means lots of repetitions)

- children not doing what you would like them to do (because they are unclear or because they think the instruction is directed at someone else)

- children ignoring the instruction all together.

Effective teachers give clear and specific instructions to children. Therefore, before you give an instruction make sure you know exactly what it is that you want the children to do, and know that it is important that they are given the instruction at that time. Sometimes we can give children instructions that involve things we want them to do later (we run the risk of them forgetting), or we give them many instructions (they might ignore the important ones).

Instructions in the classroom can take many forms and be used in different contexts. For example, you may want to give the whole class an instruction about what they need to do to get ready for a lesson. Or you may want to single out a child to tell them what they need to be doing. There are instructions that tell children what to do and there are instructions that tell children what to stop doing. Let's go through each type of instruction and look at the ways that work.

CHAPTER 4 ▓ GIVING EFFECTIVE INSTRUCTIONS AND PRAISE

Giving instructions to the whole class or small groups

Quite often in classrooms, teachers need to give the whole class or group of children an instruction. It is a common concern of teachers that they have to continually repeat themselves and spend a lot of time making sure they are heard. In my experience, these instructions are sometimes given:

(a)   when children are not listening

(b)   in a vague, non directive way

(c)   repeatedly until all children have heard the instruction.

The following steps provide some guidelines on how to give an instruction so that all children hear it and you only have to say it once.

1.   Before giving an instruction you need to have the whole class's attention.

2.   Say to the class 'Stop what you are doing and look at me'. It is important that you do not begin to give an instruction until you have the class's attention, otherwise you will have to repeat the instruction several times (which is frustrating and time consuming). Some strategies for getting the whole class's attention include:

  ▓   using a clapping signal (simple beat that all children listen to and have to join)

  ▓   putting up one hand and counting to five (children have to (1) stop talking, (2) stop what they are doing, (3) look at you, (4) put down anything in their hands and (5) listen carefully)

  ▓   having a big red stop sign that you hold up

  ▓   some other distinct signal to indicate that the class's attention is needed. I have seen teachers use whistles, but I do not encourage this as it seems to create more of a military style environment.

KIDS BEHAVING BADLY

3. Once the children are used to the signal that you use, you can very quickly gain their attention and you can tell who is not 'tuned in' by checking to see that all faces are turned towards you. Once you have all the children looking at you, then give the instruction.

4. Give the instruction clearly and specifically. Remember to keep your instructions short and succinct. For example:

   'Year 4, I want you to do two things. First, open your book and then write today's date at the top. Geoffrey, tell me what you have to do' (have a child repeat the instruction).

5. Having a child repeat the instruction lets you know if what you said was clear, and it keeps children concentrating (as they do not know if they might be the one to repeat the instruction)

6. When a few children have started to do what you have asked, begin to praise individual students for following the instruction. Make sure that you choose different children each time so that everyone receives praise at some stage.

7. If listening to instructions is a serious problem in your classroom, then you could use the token program to improve this behaviour. Children gain a reward if they stop what they are doing and look at you within a certain time period (e.g. five seconds, before the end of five claps).

Giving instructions to a child

Frequently in the classroom you need to give individual children instructions. These instructions might involve telling a child what to do, or telling a child what they should be doing instead of misbehaving. For children with short-term auditory memory difficulties, behaviour problems or attentional difficulties, following instructions can be an area of weakness. However, the following steps should be used for all children as you very quickly take the process into your general communication repertoire.

1. Get close to the child if possible. Stand near the child and turn your body towards him/her.

CHAPTER 4 ■ GIVING EFFECTIVE INSTRUCTIONS AND PRAISE

2. Say the child's name and ask him/her to look at you. This can feel a bit 'fake' at first. But once you start using this regularly it becomes second nature to you and to the children in the class. It also leaves children in no doubt that eye contact is a critical element of communication.

3. Give the instruction clearly and specifically. Remember to keep your instructions short and succinct. For example:

   'Victoria, I want you to do two things. First, put your maths book away, and then bring your spelling book to me to correct. What are the two things I want you to do?' (have child repeat the instruction).

4. When the child seems to do what you have asked, check to ensure he/she has actually done what you asked. If so, praise the child. If not, repeat the instruction.

5. If you are giving a 'stop' instruction, make sure that you tell the child what he/she should be doing instead. This ensures that the child knows exactly what he/she needs to do and teaches him/her appropriate behaviour. Often we simply tell children to stop doing something, or may only use a look or a single word. However, we really want to make sure that the child knows exactly what the appropriate behaviour is and when you expect it to be done. This increases the likelihood of the child doing the right thing in future.

   'Olivia, stop wandering around the room. Sit down at your table and finish your maths.'

Using praise in the classroom

Children typically enjoy receiving praise and positive attention from their teacher. However it is important when giving praise that the children understand which behaviour is being praised. This increases the likelihood of that behaviour occurring again in the child being praised and in the other children who observe the praise. People in general (and teachers specifically) make far more negative comments than they do positive comments. Therefore it is important that we spend some time thinking about how we go about focusing on the good behaviours.

It is a basic principle of behaviour change that behaviours that are reinforced (rewarded with something desirable to the person) are more likely to occur in the future. Praise is one of the most basic and easy to deliver reinforcements as it does not require any prior preparation or special equipment. However, praise is also something that we may not be very good at giving.

Important points to note

- Praise should be used more frequently than negative comments. As a general rule teachers should make two positive comments in the classroom to every negative or critical comment. In fact, it would be nice if in life generally we followed this rule.

- Remember, in order for children to maintain an appropriate behaviour they need to be reinforced for it (with praise, or other types of reward).

- Make sure your praise is genuine, well earned, honest and appropriate and allows children to identify the behaviour that is being praised (so they will do it again).

Delivering praise

1. Identify what a child is doing that is appropriate.

2. Tell the child specifically what you are pleased about.

    'Good girl Lesley, you are working quietly on your assignment.'

    'That is great Ken, you have put away all your books.'

    'Well done Darren, you are sitting ready for our story.'

    'Terrific Kylie, you put your hand up to ask a question.'

3. Praise should be paired with appropriate body language (smiles, eye contact, voice tone etc.).

4. Use praise frequently and consistently.

CHAPTER 4 ▨ GIVING EFFECTIVE INSTRUCTIONS AND PRAISE

5.   Make sure public praise is something that the child likes. For some children (typically older children), being praised in public is embarrassing and acts more like a punisher. That is, they will not do the right thing in future because they do not want to stand out or be identified as 'the teacher's pet'. For these children, give them praise in private (a quiet word in their ear, or a little note). Studies have been done with children of all ages that shows that they prefer praise from their teacher than praise from their peers (as long as it is delivered in a way that they prefer—i.e. either private or public depending on the child).

Once you have established a positive, friendly classroom environment through the use of class rules and reinforcement of appropriate behaviour, only then should you move on to delivering consequences for inappropriate behaviour. Why is that? If you start only using punishment you create a less positive classroom atmosphere and your focus is on eliminating undesirable behaviours rather than teaching and establishing new, desirable behaviours in the children.

38

Consequences for problem behaviours

5

CHAPTER

This section deals with how to manage behaviours that you do not want to see in your classroom. What can you do to provide consequences that are relevant and effective? Remember that graduate who to told me that she deals with behaviour problems by getting children to stand with their nose to the blackboard? Fortunately there are better, less demeaning ways to manage misbehaviour. Listed below are some ideas for you to take into your own classroom.

Establishing logical consequences in the classroom

While setting up systems that monitor and reward positive behaviours in your classroom helps to minimise problem behaviours, there will still be times when some children will behave inappropriately. When this happens you need to have clear and consistent consequences that you can use. When a child does the wrong thing, there needs to be a meaningful consequence so that they are less likely to repeat the behaviour in future. It is important to ensure the consequences are meaningful to the child and fit the behaviour. For example, if a child breaks another child's pencil, then it would appropriate for the child to give the other a new pencil.

Logical consequences require that 'the punishment fits the crime' so to speak. This might involve the child practising the appropriate behaviour or writing down what he/she should have done. Consequences can involve removal of access to a desired activity (e.g. free time or computer time). They may involve notes home to parents, or additional work.

A list of possible consequences is provided below, to give you some additional ideas. Consequences can be positive and negative and for every behaviour you are targeting, there should be a consequence. It is important that you notice the list of positive consequences that go along with these. When the child does the right thing, it is important that they are acknowledged for that as well.

CHAPTER 5 ■ CONSEQUENCES FOR PROBLEM BEHAVIOURS

EXAMPLES OF POTENTIAL CONSEQUENCES	
REWARDS FOR DOING THE RIGHT THING	CONSEQUENCES FOR NOT FOLLOWING THE RULES
Attention—praise, smiles	Practise appropriate behaviour
Stickers, stars, ticks	Change of seating
Positive notes to parents	Note to parents
Desired activity	Note from teacher
Free time	Additional work
Certificate	Removal from activity
Lollies	Extra time in class
Position of responsibility	Ignoring inappropriate behaviour
Stamp	Loss of house points
Points towards larger reward	Meeting with parents
Access to computer	Work sheets
Note from teacher	Loss of free time/part of lunch
Special book	Seating alone

Consequences need to be logically related to the behaviour and relevant to the individual child. You need to monitor whether the child's behaviour changes as a result of the consequences you choose. If a child's behaviour does not change, then you will need to try another consequence.

It is important that a consequence for inappropriate behaviour occurs for every instance of that behaviour and as close to the occurrence as possible. Remember, our aim is to teach children what to do. As a result they need to know that they are not going to get away with

41

it 'every now and then'. If this happens then it is very hard to eliminate the behaviour as the children will think 'maybe this time I will get away with it' and will take a chance with the unwanted behaviour. However, if they know that every time they do the undesirable behaviour you will notice and give a consequence, they will very quickly stop trying that behaviour.

The consequence needs to be followed by an explanation about what the appropriate behaviour should have been. They may need clear instructions on how to develop the desirable behaviour. This again ensures the child learns what to do.

For serious behaviour problems such as aggression (verbal and physical) or repeated breaches of class rules you may need stronger consequences. These could include calling the parents up to the school, loss of privileges, or principal intervention. Time-out may also be an option that can be used in your classroom.

Time-out procedures for the classroom

Time-out means time away from reinforcers—or time away from interesting things. Time-out removes the child from the attention of the rest of the class and makes it clear to the child that if they are misbehaving then they will not have as much fun as children who are doing the right things. Unfortunately, time-out often gets misused and actually ends up reinforcing undesirable behaviour. Imagine a child who is sent into the corridor for distracting other children when he should have been working. The corridor can be a very interesting place to be, people constantly going past (perhaps even stopping for a chat) and lots of displays to look at. In this situation, the child is actually getting 'time-in' and may be disruptive in future in order to get sent out of the room.

Time-out, when used appropriately, helps teachers manage children's behaviour without the teacher yelling, pleading, growling and causing great disruption to the class.

The time-out procedure is not difficult to use, and most teachers see improvement in their children's behaviour within a short time. It is however, very important that teachers adhere to the following instructions and only use time-out in conjunction with strategies that increase a child's appropriate behaviours (praise, positive reinforcement, rewards programs etc.).

CHAPTER 5 ■ CONSEQUENCES FOR PROBLEM BEHAVIOURS

Before beginning time-out

- Before using time-out check with your principal to ensure that it is acceptable for you to use a time-out area in the classroom. The time-out strategy I recommend for classrooms is non-exclusionary (i.e. the child remains in the classroom) and involves the child moving to a specified area where they are separated from other children for a short amount of time. It is may also be important to tell parents about this strategy so that they understand how it will work. Parents may have very different ideas on what time-out involves, so providing this information should clear up any concerns about the child's safety and learning opportunities.

- I do not recommend time-out where a child is sent from a classroom. Apart from this possibly being rewarding for the child, it is often not safe as the child can not be easily supervised.

The time-out area

- The time-out area does not have to be outside the classroom, as it has been suggested in the past. In fact it is preferable that the time-out area is within the classroom so that the teacher can monitor the child and to ensure the child remains in the time-out area.

- The time-out area should be an uninteresting and dull place. Remember that you are removing the child from a reinforcing and interesting environment, so do not remove him/her to another reinforcing environment (e.g. near the door where he/she can watch the comings and goings). The child must find the time-out area to be less stimulating than what they were doing.

- Depending on the year level, the time-out area could be a mat on the floor or a table set apart from the other tables. It is important that the table/mat is placed in such a way that the child will not be able to see the other children when placed in the time-out area. Teachers often place the table facing a wall or facing the away from the other tables.

- The use of a kitchen timer or stopwatch is useful for keeping track of the time-out period. The optimal period for a child to be placed in time-out is around one minute

43

for each year of their life (up to a **maximum of 10 minutes**). Time-out should not involve long periods of time as children forget why they are there and have reduced opportunity to learn appropriate behaviours.

Implementing time-out

1. Before implementing time-out you should explain to your class what is expected as well as the consequences of misbehaviour. As already mentioned, it is a very good idea to establish class rules (see page 20) at the beginning of the year. These are standard and important rules that are to be followed and may lead to time-out or other consequences if disobeyed repeatedly.

2. Explain to the class that when someone is in time-out the rest of the class is not allowed to talk to him/her or give him/her any attention. It needs to be made clear to the class that this is not somewhere they want to go.

3. Instructions must provide specific information about what the child is to do or is to stop doing e.g. 'Jenny, please stop throwing things at Tran now'.

4. Provide a time-out warning. If the child does not obey your request, warn him/her once that continued non-compliance will lead to time-out. Do not raise your voice. The warning is given firmly but not yelled.

    - The time-out warning gives the child the opportunity to do the right thing.

    - If a child is aggressive toward another child or demonstrates a serious behaviour problem then do not give a warning, but instead implement time-out immediately. If a child knows he/she will get a warning each time then he might use that as an opportunity to hit out knowing he/she won't get into trouble until he/she does it again!

5. If, after the warning the child does not do what you told him/her to, then he/she is sent to the time-out spot. This should be done without yelling and without further explanation. Simply say, 'Mark, we do not have that sort of behaviour here. You must go to time-out now'. Once the child is seated in the time-out area and is quiet, start the clock.

CHAPTER 5 ■ CONSEQUENCES FOR PROBLEM BEHAVIOURS

6. It is a good idea to have the child take his/her work with him/her into the Time-Out area. In addition, having easy access to some worksheets (that do not require teacher explanation) is useful if the child is sent to time-out during an activity when they are not working on a specific task. We do not want the time-out area to be a place where children can avoid doing work, as this might then become somewhere they try to be sent (we always have to be one step ahead of them).

7. If you have placed a child in time-out for failure to perform a task, do not complete the task yourself (or have other children do it) while the child is in time-out. As soon as time-out is ended, ask the child to perform the task. If he/she refuses, immediately return him/her back to time-out.

8. If a child will not do a task after repeated time-out sessions then you need to use an even more serious consequence. This might involve sending a note home to the child's parents, setting additional work, having the child stay in at lunch time etc.

REMEMBER: the period of time-out is to be a period of non-disruption, therefore the child must sit quietly for the required time. The time does not start until he is quiet.

What if a child refuses to go to time-out?

When a child refuses to go to time-out simply and calmly inform the child that the time-out period will be doubled. This also goes for disobedience during time-out. Once you have doubled the time-out period, any further disruptions should result in you forwarding a letter home to the parents.

What if a child leaves the time-out area?

Each time a child leaves the time-out area, inform him/her that you are going to start time-out again. If you can't get the child to stay in the time-out area then use a more serious consequence such as those suggested above.

Summary

The time-out procedure is very effective if it is used consistently and calmly and if you follow the directions exactly. Children will soon learn that it is easier to obey teacher requests than to go to time-out.

By this point in the book you should have established good classroom management strategies where you have effective instructions, clear rules, reinforcement for appropriate behaviour and consequences for inappropriate behaviour. The next section deals with those commonly occurring behaviour problems that we talked about at the beginning and provides some step-by-step ideas for managing these behaviours. These are presented in the form of tip sheets that you can quickly refer to without having to reread the whole book.

Specific behaviour problems—using the teacher tip sheets

6

Once you have established positive approaches to general classroom management you should be spending less time dealing with disruptive behaviour. However, there are likely to be children who still demonstrate some inappropriate behaviours that require particular attention. This section provides you with tip sheets for those minor problem behaviours that are frequently seen in the classroom. The tip sheets are recommended for use with primary school children who demonstrate any of the seven specific behaviour problems in the classroom: talking out of turn, hindering other children, aggression, poor social skills, disorganisation, withdrawal, and being off task. The tip sheets are most effective when the child's behaviour is not severe (in which case referral to a clinical setting might be warranted) and when the teacher follows exactly the steps outlined in the tip sheets.

Generally teachers have reported that these tip sheets provide commonsense procedures that can work effectively when appropriately implemented in the classroom. The strategies in the tip sheets may not work for all children, and it is recommended that if you have a child with serious behaviour problems you consult with your school guidance officer before implementing any program.

These tip sheets should be used in conjunction with the classroom management strategies mentioned earlier in this book. I want to emphasise that these tip sheets will not work if you do not have some level of control in your classroom.

So how do you go about using the tip sheets? Regardless of which behaviour you are focusing on, you should follow the following steps. Firstly, you need to determine what the behaviour problem involves for that child—where, when and how often does the child exhibit the behaviour. Then you need to set up a way of monitoring this behaviour, so that when you start using the strategies you can see whether they are working. Finally, you need to have a go at using the strategies found in the tip sheets that are provided at the end of this chapter.

1. Identify the problem

Before beginning any intervention it is important to examine the child's behaviour in terms of how often he/she does the inappropriate behaviour and if there are any patterns to when or why the child does it. This information is called the *baseline data*. Baseline data provides you with a standard to which you can compare the child's behaviour after you have introduced the intervention. It allows you to identify quickly if there are any problems

CHAPTER 6 ▨ SPECIFIC BEHAVIOUR PROBLEMS—USING THE TEACHER TIP SHEETS

with the intervention, by looking at whether the child's behaviour has continued to be a problem at the same level or a higher level than baseline.

(a) Define the problem behaviour in operational terms (i.e. in a way that can be measured)

Each of the teacher tip sheets provides an intervention strategy for a specific behavioural problem. Each behavioural problem has been described, however you will need to be more specific about exactly what you will measure to determine outcome.

For example, when working with a withdrawn child you might want to measure how social the child is with other children. With this description alone, you could be measuring a whole range of behaviours (talking to others, talking to the teacher, time spent with other children, social initiations etc.). Therefore, pick one specific behaviour to measure— e.g. initiating conversation with the teacher or other children in the classroom.

Most of the tip sheets target behaviours that are easy to measure. It is recommended that the following discrete behaviours are monitored:

- **Talking out of turn**—This will require tallying the number of times the child talks/calls out when it is not his/her turn.

- **Hindering other children**—This will require tallying the number of times the child disrupts other children during learning times (talking to or physically interfering with other children).

- **Poor social skills**—This will require you to determine the main social problem of the child (i.e. is it that the child does not talk to others, does not share, does not look people in the eye, etc.?).

- **Withdrawn children**—This involves recording the number of times the child initiates conversation/comments to other children or to the teacher.

- **Aggression**—This involves recording the number of times the child is physically aggressive towards other children (hits, pokes, kicks, touches inappropriately).

KIDS BEHAVING BADLY

- **Disorganised children**—This will require tallying the number of times the teacher has to remind the child to remember items, number of times the child brings/uses the wrong books, etc.

- **Keeping on task**—This involves recording the number of times the teacher has to remind the child to return to his/her work.

(b) Collect information about the frequency and intensity of the problem

Once you have decided on the specific behaviour that you will be measuring, you are ready to begin collecting the baseline data.

Usually two weeks of baseline data is recommended, as this will give you a relatively stable picture of the level of the child's problem behaviour. While this might seem like a waste of your time, it really is important as it helps you to get an idea of where, when and how frequently the child does the behaviour. Also it allows you to monitor the progress you make once you start using the strategies outlined on the relevant tip sheet.

Using the daily record form

Using the daily record of child behaviour (found on page 52), first familiarise yourself with the recording technique. Place the recording sheet where the children will not see it, but somewhere that you can easily access it—perhaps on a clipboard or on your desk.

On the daily record form the school day is divided into three sessions. If you are not able to record the child's behaviour in a session (e.g. if the child is in a specialist class, is being taught by someone else, or you are not present), put a cross through that session. This is important otherwise, it will look as if the child has not shown the problem behaviour during that time.

CHAPTER 6 ▓ SPECIFIC BEHAVIOUR PROBLEMS—USING THE TEACHER TIP SHEETS

SAMPLE RECORD FORM FOR TALKING OUT OF TURN					
PERIOD	**MONDAY**	**TUESDAY**	**WEDNESDAY**	**THURSDAY**	**FRIDAY**
Morning (before recess)	IIII	IIIII	II	Not in classroom	III
Midmorning (after recess)	Not in classroom	III	IIIII	IIIIII	IIIII
Afternoon (after lunch)	IIIIII	IIII	Not in classroom	IIIIII	Not in classroom
Average per session per day (total/sessions)	5	4	3.5	6	4

Every time the child exhibits the specific behaviour make a mark on record sheet in the appropriate session. Some teachers have found it easier to discretely make a mark on their hand or on a small piece of paper and then transfer this to the record sheet at the end of the session.

NB: It is important that the child and other children are not aware that you are recording.

KIDS BEHAVING BADLY

TEACHER DAILY RECORD FORM

Teacher's name: Week number:

Record of child's behaviour

Whenever the child does the undesirable behaviour place a tick in the appropriate time period. At the end of the day, total the number of times for the whole day and divide by the number of sessions.

PERIOD	MONDAY	TUESDAY	WEDNESDAY	THURSDAY	FRIDAY
Morning (before recess)					
Midmorning (after recess)					
Afternoon (after lunch)					
Average per session per day (total/sessions)					

CHAPTER 6 ■ SPECIFIC BEHAVIOUR PROBLEMS—USING THE TEACHER TIP SHEETS

Graph the results

At the end of the day, total the number of times the child did the inappropriate behaviour and divide this by the number of sessions in which the behaviour was recorded. This will give you an average occurrence per session for each day.

Transfer this average occurrence onto the graph provided (on page 54). After two weeks you will have 10 points on the graph that you can then use to compare the child's behaviour following intervention. Below is an example of such a graph.

Example:

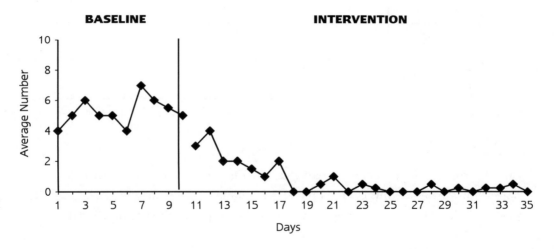

The first part of the graph is the baseline period, where the teacher has just recorded how often the child talked out of turn. This gave the teacher a good idea of how much of a problem this was, as it can be seen that on day seven the child talked out of turn an average of seven times per session (this is a real example where a session was around one hour long—the poor teacher)! Once the teacher started using the intervention, the child's talking out of turn began to decrease and by the end of the recording the child was calling out rarely if at all.

KIDS BEHAVING BADLY

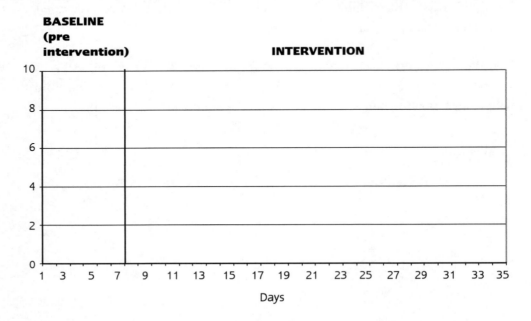

GRAPH OF BEHAVIOUR CHANGE

Child's name: Behaviour targeted:

Instructions: At the end of each day, total the number of times the child did the inappropriate behaviour. Divide this by the number of sessions in which recording took place. Mark this session average number on the graph for the appropriate day.

CHAPTER 6 ▓ SPECIFIC BEHAVIOUR PROBLEMS—USING THE TEACHER TIP SHEETS

2. Implement the intervention

(a) Familiarise yourself with the tip sheet

Take some time to read the tip sheet and familiarise yourself with the steps involved. Make sure you know what you will do as soon as the child demonstrates the problem behaviour, and the exact consequences you will use.

(b) Decide on the consequences

You can decide the most appropriate reinforcements and punishers for the individual child. It is important to ensure the consequences are meaningful to the child. For example, a child who is extremely shy may not like to be praised in front of the whole class. In this case it would be wiser to reinforce the child's behaviour with a quiet word or a note home to his/her parents.

Some examples of consequences are provided on each of the tip sheets (and also on page 41), however you can alter these to suit the individual child and classroom. A list of potential consequences is provided below, to give you some additional ideas. However, it is important to monitor whether the child's behaviour responds to the use of the consequences you choose. If a child's behaviour does not change, then you will need to try another consequence.

55

POSSIBLE CONSEQUENCES
Withdraw attention for behaviour
Change of seating
Note to parents
Note from teacher
Additional work
Removal from activity
Extra time in class
Practice appropriate behaviour
Loss of house points
Meeting with parents
Work sheets
Loss of free time/part of lunch
Seating alone

Once you are familiar with the tip sheet and have your consequences organised, you are ready to implement the tip sheet strategies. Often consequences are negotiated with the class at the beginning of the year, as discussed earlier in the book.

(c) Implement the strategies

The strategies in the tip sheet can be used for the whole class. In fact, our research has demonstrated that even when the strategies were used with one individual child, other children in the class also started changing their behaviour (Little, Hudson & Wilks 2002).

The strategies in the tip sheet need to be implemented consistently and continuously. While it may feel unnatural to start with, it is necessary for the child to receive

CHAPTER 6 ■ SPECIFIC BEHAVIOUR PROBLEMS—USING THE TEACHER TIP SHEETS

reinforcement every time he/she does the right thing. Once the child starts demonstrating the appropriate behaviour on a regular basis, you can begin to progressively increase the period between reinforcement (e.g. every second time the child does the appropriate behaviour and gradually increasing this so the reinforcement occurs more randomly). However, the consequences set out in the tip sheet must occur for every incident of the problem behaviour, otherwise the child may return to the baseline levels of the behaviour.

(d) Graph the results and monitor progress

Continue to record the child's behaviour for four weeks, graphing the daily average as you go. Monitor the graph to ensure that the changes in the child's behaviour are occurring as desired (i.e. if you want the behaviour to decrease then the line on the graph should continue to head towards zero).

With some behaviours there might be an initial increase in the inappropriate behaviour as the child tries to get the attention he used to get for that behaviour. This will be particularly evident when you are using a strategy that involves ignoring a behaviour (the child might talk more/yell louder to get your attention). It is important that you continue to implement the appropriate consequences as outlined in the tip sheet.

If the child's behaviour stays at the same level as at baseline, or worsens over a number of days, then you may need to review the tip sheet program. Is there something that you are not doing? Is there something that has changed in the classroom? Is there anything else going on with the child? If you have been implementing the tip sheet as advised and the child's behaviour has worsened then you may need to consider more intensive assistance. Contact your school psychologist or student welfare co-ordinator for further advice on behaviour management strategies.

3. Plan for maintenance of appropriate behaviour

Once the child's new behaviour appears to be stable (after 4–6 weeks), you can stop recording the behaviour if you wish. It is still important to monitor the child's progress and return to continuous reinforcement of the appropriate behaviour if the child seems to be returning to his/her old ways. Once again, the consequences for inappropriate behaviour should continue to be used so that the child is aware that if he/she does the 'wrong thing' then he/she will be presented with a certain consequence.

4. Do a follow-up in three months

Recording the child's behaviour three months after finishing the formal intervention can provide you with valuable information about the effectiveness of the intervention. If the child has continued to behave appropriately then this reassures you that the program has continued to work over time. If however, the child's behaviour has worsened again, then you need to consider whether the consequences have been used consistently and appropriately. You may need to return to the start of intervention again to 'remind' the child of the behaviours that are expected.

Summary

These tip sheets are not designed to replace consultation with a psychologist, they are designed to provide teachers with effective strategies to deal with minor behaviour problems. If you are concerned about the seriousness of a child's behaviour, contact your school's guidance officer for further assistance.

The tip sheets can be found on the following pages. These are then followed by a section that deals with getting parents involved in changing a child's behaviour. This may include involving parents with the implementation of specific strategies for a behaviour. It is also important to get parents involved generally in behaviour management, for both appropriate and inappropriate child behaviour.

Talking out of turn

Children sometimes talk out of turn in class, an action that can disrupt the flow of a lesson and interfere with other children's learning. If not addressed, this kind of behaviour can worsen and become a habit for the child. This tip sheet gives some suggestions to help you teach your children not to talk out of turn.

Talking out of turn is one of the classroom problems that teachers most often report. It is a major problem because the learning of other children may be affected. Simply ignoring this behaviour may not be effective in stopping the child talking out of turn. These suggestions are designed to be used when the child is required to take turns in answering questions.

Why do children talk out of turn?

Children may talk out of turn for a number of reasons. Children may talk out of turn in lessons because they are worried that if they don't respond immediately they will forget their thought. Alternatively, some children may enjoy the attention they gain from speaking out of turn (from both the teacher and other children). Even being reprimanded can be rewarding for some children. Another possibility is that the child has not yet learnt to wait to be asked to respond.

Preventing talking out of turn

Explain answering procedure to the class

Teach the children how you expect them to respond to your questions or during lessons (putting hands up, not calling out, listening to others etc.). Ideally this should be done at the start of the year as class rules, but will still be beneficial throughout the year. Have them practise responding during a 'mock' lesson. Respond positively to all children who wait their turn before speaking.

Establish a response time

Teach children to count silently to 5 before raising their hand. This encourages them to think about their response and restricts impulsive responding.

Praise the child for waiting

When you observe the child awaiting his/her turn before speaking, give him/her praise. Praising other children who wait will teach children that they will get more attention for waiting than for talking out of turn.

Make the delays manageable

For the child who has a difficulty waiting, begin by making him/her wait only a short time before asking him/her to respond (e.g. asking them second). When he/she responds at the appropriate time, praise him/her for waiting. Say something like—*Good girl Lisa, you waited until I asked you.*

CHAPTER 6 ■ SPECIFIC BEHAVIOUR PROBLEMS—USING THE TEACHER TIP SHEETS

When he/she is able to wait that short time, you can then gradually increase the amount of time he/she has to wait (e.g. asking them third, then fourth and so on).

Encourage children to display the appropriate behaviour

Remind all children of how you wish them to behave while waiting to respond (rather than making an example of one child). Continue to praise all children (at various times) for waiting their turn.

When a child does talk out of turn

The first time: tell the child what to do

The first time the behaviour occurs in a lesson—speak firmly and tell the child what to do instead of talking out of turn. Say something like—*Sarah, don't talk out of turn. Put your hand up and wait quietly.* Try to praise the child for appropriate behaviour shortly after this incident.

The second time: provide a consequence

The second and following times the child calls out in a lesson, provide a consequence. Say something like—*Paul, you are still not waiting your turn. You will complete this worksheet after the lesson.* It is important that the child does not use talking out of turn to avoid lessons; therefore, the consequence needs to occur immediately after the lesson has been completed.

Allow practice

Each lesson is an opportunity for children to practise waiting before responding, and plenty of praise should be given each time the child waits before responding.

Key steps

- ▦ Teach the whole class appropriate behaviour.

- ▦ Praise the child for waiting to be asked before speaking.

- ▦ Make the waiting time manageable for the child.

- ▦ When the child talks out of turn take action straight away.

- ▦ The first time it occurs: remind the child of the appropriate behaviour.

- ▦ The second and subsequent times: use a consequence.

- ▦ Give the child plenty of opportunities for practice.

Hindering other children

Children sometimes use class time to interfere with other children's learning. This may involve talking to other children, acting out, continually borrowing things and generally drawing attention to themselves. If not dealt with, this kind of behaviour can get worse and become a habit for the child. This tip sheet gives some suggestions to help you teach your children not to hinder others.

Hindering other children is one of the most commonly reported classroom problems. It is a major problem because the learning of other children may be affected. Simply ignoring this behaviour may result in children becoming more intrusive in their efforts to interfere with the learning process. These suggestions can be used when a child is supposed to be working quietly and independently, or when working within a group.

Why do children hinder others?

Children may hinder others for a number of reasons. Children may do this as a way to avoid working. The child may be unsure of the requirements and need to check with another child. The child may be disorganised and not have the necessary materials. Children may enjoy the attention (from both the teacher and other children). Even reprimands can be rewarding for some children.

Preventing children from interrupting others

Explain appropriate behaviour to the class

Teach the children how you expect them to behave during class time. Ideally this should be done at the start of the year, but will still be beneficial throughout the year. Class rules can be very useful.

Write down steps

Write down the steps involved in the learning task, ask children to repeat these steps and make sure they have the necessary equipment before they start. Respond positively to all children who start quickly and quietly.

Establish a procedure for questions

Teach the children to raise their hands when they are unsure of something (so they ask you rather than other children). Teach children to count silently to 5 before raising their hand. This encourages them to think about their response and restricts impulsive responding.

Time-out table

Place a table near you, where a child who is disturbing others can be seated for a short period of time. While it is often thought that this may damage a child's confidence, research clearly demonstrates that this is not the case. In the long run the child learns valuable skills in controlling his/her behaviour.

CHAPTER 6 ▪ SPECIFIC BEHAVIOUR PROBLEMS—USING THE TEACHER TIP SHEETS

Praise children for working quietly

When you observe the child working quietly, give him/her a lot of praise. Praising other children who work without hindering others will teach the children that they will obtain more attention for this than for disturbing other children.

Do not wait for the child to be disruptive before providing attention; provide plenty of attention for appropriate work behaviour.

Remind children to display the appropriate behaviour

Periodically remind the class of how you wish them to behave while working (rather than making an example of one child).

When a child does disturb others

The first time: tell the child what to do

Speak firmly and tell the child what to do instead of disturbing other children. Say something like—*Cathy, don't talk to Sam. Put your hand up and ask me, or work quietly.* Once the child is working appropriately, provide praise for the behaviour.

The second time: provide a consequence

The second and subsequent times in a lesson that the child disturbs others, provide the consequence (e.g. moving the child). Say something like—*Paul, you are still disturbing the class. You will sit at the front table for 10 minutes.* This consequence should be provided as soon as you see the child disturbing others. The longer it is delayed, the more learning time is affected.

Once the child has returned to his/her seat, praise appropriate working behaviour. If he/she disturbs others again provide the same consequence. If this behaviour occurs more than three times during a lesson, provide a stronger consequence. This may involve a letter home to the child's parents, extra homework, or staying in for part of lunch/recess.

Key steps

- Teach the whole class appropriate behaviour.

- Write down all the steps and the equipment needed where it can be easily read by the child.

- Praise the child for working without disturbing others.

- When the child disturbs others take action immediately.

- Remind the child of the appropriate behaviour.

- If the child continues to disrupt, use a consequence such as removal to the front table (with their back to other children) for a short period of time.

- Give the child plenty of opportunities for practice.

63

Keeping on task

Children sometimes have difficulty keeping on task and completing work. If not addressed, this kind of behaviour can get worse and result in children falling behind with their work. This tip sheet gives some suggestions to help you keep your children on task.

On-task time directly affects learning outcomes. Therefore, it is important that children are focused and able to concentrate on their work in class. If children are off task, not only is their learning likely to suffer, so too is the work of those around them. By reinforcing children for being on task, much of the off-task behaviour may be reduced. These strategies can be used for 'silent' work times, and also for group work times when the child needs to be on task.

Reasons for off-task behaviour

Children may have difficulty concentrating for a number of reasons. They may have difficulty focusing on the important aspects of the task. Alternatively, some children may find it difficult to stick to a task that they find uninteresting. Some children may find the work too difficult. Others may simply enjoy the social aspects of being off task.

Children with a diagnosis of ADHD are particularly prone to being off task and will benefit from a very structured approach to learning.

Preventing off-task behaviour

Tell the children the day's schedule. Letting children know in advance what is coming up allows them plenty of time to understand what they are expected to do.

Gain eye contact

When you are teaching the children a new concept, having eye contact with all children allows you to monitor which children are concentrating.

Keep up the pace

Lessons should be paced so that children do not have time be distracted or bored. Making the lessons interactive with random questions (instead of asking for volunteer answers), will keep the children alert.

Write down the steps involved

Writing down the requirements of the task where children can easily see them will increase the likelihood that the children know what they are required to do.

Keep on the move

Children are more likely to stay on task when they know the teacher is monitoring the class. When you walk around, the child can never be sure when you will observe him/her next.

CHAPTER 6 ■ SPECIFIC BEHAVIOUR PROBLEMS—USING THE TEACHER TIP SHEETS

Modify tasks

For children who have difficulty staying on task and completing work, task modification may be needed. Giving them a reduced amount of work will make the task more manageable and increase the likelihood of their successfully finishing the task in the allocated time. As their concentration time improves the tasks can gradually be made longer. This will need to be done privately, as other children may complain. Simply drawing a line on a worksheet indicating where the child should reach in the lesson is a simple way of modifying tasks.

Encourage the child for working

When you observe the child on task, give him/her a lot of praise. Praising other children who are also on task will teach the children that they will get more attention for staying on task than for being off task.

When a child is off task

Act quickly

As soon as you observe restlessness in children, move close to them and monitor their work.

Tell the child what to do

Speak firmly and cue the child into what he should be doing. Say something like—*Shane, you still need to answer your maths questions.* Once the child has settled back to work, find an opportunity to praise the child for being on task.

Rewards for completion of work

Allow children who finish their work to have access to a desired activity. By shortening the child's work task into a manageable

concentration time, he will soon be able to concentrate for longer periods of time if his behaviour is rewarded.

Consequences for incomplete work

Once you have to remind the child a *second* time to be on task during a lesson, provide a consequence for the behaviour. Say something like—*Emily, you will stay in your seat until you have finished that worksheet.* Any work that is not completed in class time should be completed at recess, or sent home to be completed during free time. Sometimes parents can be relied on to ensure the child completes the work instead of engaging in a favoured activity (e.g. a tv program).

Praise often for on-task behaviour

Catching children on task and praising them frequently demonstrates that you are aware of their behaviour and appreciate the efforts they make.

Key steps

- Let children know in advance what they will be doing.

- Monitor children visually, and continually walk around during work time.

- Make the tasks manageable for the distractible child.

- Praise and reward children for on-task behaviour.

- If you have to give a second reminder, use a consequence.

- Give the child plenty of opportunities to be praised for on-task behaviour.

65

Poor social skills

Some children lack the necessary skills for making friends, interacting with others and communicating their needs. These children may be isolated, attention seeking, may have academic difficulties and may feel rejected by their peers. This tip sheet gives some suggestions to help you assist children with poor social skills.

Social skills are vital for children as these are the behaviours they need to make and keep friends, to get on with others and to feel happy and accepted at school. Developing positive communication skills will benefit school age children in all aspects of their social interactions, as these are skills needed every day at every age.

Why some children lack social skills

Children may lack social skills because they have not had the opportunity to observe and practise appropriate social interactions, they might lack confidence, or they may feel self conscious about some aspect of themselves.

How to teach appropriate social skills

Teach the whole class social skills

Teaching socially appropriate behaviours such as communication skills, sharing and problem solving as a lesson might prevent problems occurring.

It may also teach other children to be more accepting of children who are different. *Friendly Kids: Friendly Classrooms* by Helen McGrath and Shona Francey (1991) deals with classroom-based approaches to developing appropriate behaviours.

Place the child with friendly children

Seating the child with children who have good social skills will expose the child to appropriate ways of interacting.

Model appropriate behaviour

Show the children how to interact with others by demonstrating appropriate behaviour. During lesson times, take opportunities to ask children for things and highlight the important features of your request. Say something like—*Class, I want you to notice how I ask Jacob for something.* This will cue all children into appropriate communication.

Provide opportunities for social skills

Use group work as times for the child to practise interacting with others. Give each child a role, so all children must contribute. Praise children for interacting well with others. Say something like—*I really liked the way you looked at Tracey when you asked her that question.* Do this for all children so that the target child does not feel singled out.

CHAPTER 6 ■ SPECIFIC BEHAVIOUR PROBLEMS—USING THE TEACHER TIP SHEETS

Select working groups yourself

Pair up children yourself when required for work or games. This will prevent one child being excluded by others. Pairing the child lacking in social skills with a more social child will encourage the child to observe and practise social skills.

Alternatively, make it a class rule that each child must work with a different partner for each new groupwork activity. This will encourage all children to develop social skills by working with people they are not so familiar with.

Encourage problem solving

Teach children strategies for problem situations. For example, with teasing you could set up role plays in class where various children have to think of strategies for dealing with this (ensuring that you do not identify children who are experiencing this problem—i.e. make it a general activity).

Encourage activities that include all children both in the class and during lunch time (if possible).

When the child uses inappropriate social skills

When you observe the child interacting poorly, tell the child the correct way to behave. Say something like—*Kemal, look at Tim and ask him to pass you the pencils.*

Praise the child for appropriate behaviour.

Talk with other teachers

Find out if there are other children with social skills problems in other classes.

It may be useful to discuss with the principal the possibility of setting up a social skills program across the school. The *Friendly Kids: Friendly Classrooms* book (McGrath & Francey 1991) has intervention strategies that can be used with small groups or whole classes.

Key steps

- Teach the whole class appropriate behaviour.
- Model good social skills.
- Place the child with more socially adept children.
- Praise and reward children for appropriate social behaviour.
- Encourage problem solving.
- Establish social skills groups if needed.

For social skills problems that are serious or ongoing, contact your school's guidance officer.

KIDS BEHAVING BADLY

Aggression

Children sometimes will hurt other children at school. They may hit, pull hair, push or scratch. If not dealt with, this kind of behaviour can get worse. This tip sheet gives some suggestions to help reduce aggression.

Aggressive behaviours can take a number of forms including physical behaviours and verbal behaviour (name calling, swearing). Ignoring these behaviours can result in the aggression becoming worse. By developing positive communication skills in addition to consequences for aggression, change can be made in the aggressive child.

Why are children aggressive?

Children may be aggressive for a number of reasons. Hurting others typically gets a big reaction from the victims, which may encourage the child to keep hurting others. The child may not have the appropriate communication skills to gain what he/she wants and may use aggression to get things. Children may hurt others out of frustration because they are not getting their own way. Some children may be aggressive because they have had this sort of behaviour modelled for them (from television, siblings, relatives or peers).

Prevention of aggression

Teach the whole class appropriate behaviour

Teaching socially appropriate behaviours such as communication skills, sharing and problem solving as a lesson might prevent some problems occurring. *Friendly Kids: Friendly Classrooms* by Helen McGrath and Shona Francey (1991) deals with classroom-based approaches to developing appropriate behaviours.

Have a 'time-out' area

Have a table or mat at the front of the room, where a child can be sent following aggressive behaviour. Ideally this should be located so the child can not see the other children.

Monitor the child

Try to monitor the child at times when he/she is typically aggressive. This may be much easier to do in the classroom than in the playground. It might be a good idea to talk to yard duty staff and have them keep an eye out for the child. Speedy intervention is needed when a child is about to hurt someone.

Encourage appropriate behaviour

When you catch the child being 'good' give a lot of praise; state the reason for the praise. Say— *Good Sam. You are sharing with Tim.*

CHAPTER 6 ▪ SPECIFIC BEHAVIOUR PROBLEMS—USING THE TEACHER TIP SHEETS

When a child is aggressive

The first time: act quickly when a child hurts another child or is aggressive. Speak firmly and tell the child what to do instead of being aggressive. *Claire, ask Mark for your pencil back. Don't hit him.* Then provide a consequence for the behaviour. *Claire, you hurt Mark. Go and sit on the mat at the front of the room and finish your work.* Set a short amount of time that the child must stay in that seat being quiet (a maximum of 10 minutes).

Practise appropriate behaviour

The next step is to show the child how to interact with the other child. For example, ask for a turn instead of pushing, tell the teacher when someone hurts them first, or count to 10 before acting.

Subsequent aggression

The next time the child hurt others and is aggressive, provide the consequence for that behaviour. Say something like—*Marco, you are still hurting Lauren. Go and sit on the mat at the front of the room and finish your work.* Once again, set a short amount of time that the child must stay in that seat being quiet (a maximum of 10 minutes).

In the playground teachers could have the child walk around with them for a specified period of time. It is important that the child does not see this as being fun (thus no attention should be given). Similarly, the teacher should not spend the time criticising the child for his behaviour. This should be a 'quiet time'.

Allow the child to return to his seat/activity

When the time is up, allow the child to return to what she/he was doing in order for the child to practise interacting without being aggressive.

If the behaviour occurs a third time, provide a more serious consequence such as a letter home to the child's parents, keeping him in at recess, extra work and so forth.

Enlist the help of parents

If a child continues to be aggressive, enlist the help of his/her parents. Set up a daily book that goes home to the parents, writing in it instances of good behaviour as well as aggressive behaviour. Have the parents reward the good behaviour at school with a special treat.

Key steps

▪ Teach the whole class appropriate behaviour.

▪ Establish a 'time-out' area.

▪ Monitor the child at potential problem times.

▪ Praise and reward children for nonaggressive behaviour.

▪ Act swiftly when a child is aggressive. Explain what to do instead of being aggressive.

▪ Provide a consequence for the aggressive behaviour immediately.

▪ Allow the child to return to his/her activity/seat once the time out has ceased.

▪ Praise the child for any attempts at appropriate social behaviour.

For aggression problems that are more serious or extended, contact your school's guidance officer.

KIDS BEHAVING BADLY

Withdrawn children

Some children seem to have great difficulty talking in class, responding to questions and being involved in activities. These children may be isolated, shy, lack confidence and may feel rejected by their peers. This tip sheet gives some suggestions to help you assist children who are quiet and withdrawn.

Withdrawn children are not usually behaviour problems for teachers. Typically, such children may not draw attention to themselves and cause concern because of a lack of involvement in classroom activities. These children may worry a lot and lack confidence, therefore addressing these issues may result in a happier more confident children.

Why are children withdrawn?

Children may be withdrawn at school for any number of reasons. Perhaps the children worry a lot, lack confidence, are shy, are thinking about other things going on in their life, or perhaps they do not like attending school. Whatever the reason, it is important that all children interact at school as this is how vital social skills are learnt.

How to help withdrawn children

Talk with the child

Choose a time when other children are not around, and ask about any worries that he would like to talk about. Perhaps by doing this the child may feel willing to approach you with any problems. Being supportive of the child and admitting that you wonder why the child is very quiet at school may allow a discussion of any concerns. Such discussions will be most likely to occur if you have a warm and trusting relationship with your children.

Is this a recent change?

Has the child always been like this? If so, it is may be low self confidence and shyness that are causing such withdrawn behaviour. If past teachers have not reported such behaviour, a meeting with the child's parents may clarify any triggering events.

Teach good listening skills

Work with the class on listening to other people. Children take turns in practising sitting while someone speaks, then asking good questions. This will create a supportive environment for all children to speak without fear of criticism.

Seat the child with friendly children

Children who feel secure about their position are likely to interact with other children. Placing a child with very boisterous children may cause him/her to remain unnoticed. The child is better placed with children who will be friendly towards him/her. Make sure that the child is not with a friend who talks for them.

70

CHAPTER 6 ■ SPECIFIC BEHAVIOUR PROBLEMS—USING THE TEACHER TIP SHEETS

Encourage discussion in small group work

Give each child a role in group work so that she/he is required to convey information to the other children. Start off with pairs and build up to larger groups. When the child does speak, provide a quiet word of praise (too much attention might scare him/her away).

Ask the child easy questions

During lessons, ask the quiet/withdrawn child to answer easy questions (that you are sure she/he knows) to increase the number of positive experiences of responding. Praise the child for correct responses.

Give the child a responsibility

If you have special jobs in the class, try to give the child a turn at one. This will encourage a sense of responsibility and may increase her/his confidence.

Ask the child to come and tell you one interesting thing each day. This will encourage the child to initiate conversation.

Expect responses from the child

Often withdrawn children have learnt that if they take a long time in responding, the teacher might not wait (they then are being rewarded for avoiding responding). Therefore, be patient and demonstrate to the child that you will wait for an answer. The child will soon learn that it is easier to speak up quickly and confidently than take a long time and attract more attention.

Student journals

Have the children write in journals that they hand in to you. Allow them to write about anything and stress that you will be the only one reading them. This may provide the child with an outlet to express themselves. This also gives you an opportunity to get to know the child a little better.

Monitor the child

If you believe that the child is becoming more withdrawn, or that this behaviour is seriously affecting school work and social interactions then set up a discussion time with parents. This child may need more intensive assistance.

Key steps

■ Try to determine any underlying reason for the child being withdrawn.

■ Teach the whole class listening skills.

■ Build the child's confidence at participating by beginning with small groups and work up.

■ Give the child a responsibility

■ Expect responses from the child.

■ Have the child keep a journal.

■ Seek further assistance if necessary.

For withdrawn children whose behaviour does not respond to these suggestions, contact your school's guidance officer.

Disorganised children

Some children have difficulty being organised and starting their work. Such children can be very disruptive and their learning may be affected. Their behaviour can be very frustrating for their teacher because of the need to repeat instructions for individual children. This tip sheet gives some suggestions to help you improve children's personal organisation.

On-task time directly affects learning outcomes. Therefore, it is important that children are focused and able to concentrate on their work in class. If children are disorganised, not only is their learning likely to suffer, so too is the work of those nearby. By establishing routines for these children, much of their disorganisation may be reduced.

Why are children disorganised?

Children may be disorganised for a number of reasons. They may not listen to instructions, be forgetful, or be untidy. These children may be characterised by messy desks or bags, they may frequently lose things, and may need to be told things a number of times.

Preventing disorganisation

Tell the children the day's schedule

This gives children an opportunity to prepare for upcoming classes. Make a list of the books/equipment needed for each lesson and display it in the classroom.

Colour code books

If the child has a number of workbooks to be used, have a parent cover each one in a different colour paper. Then paste a key to the colours on the child's desk so the book can be found quickly for a particular lesson.

Child repeats instructions

Give the child short instructions with only one or two directions. Have the child repeat the instruction back to you to ensure understanding.

Write down the steps involved

Writing down the requirements of the task where children can easily see them will increase the likelihood that they know what they have to do.

Encourage organised behaviour

Praise children when they successfully follow instructions, or when they are organised. Have spot desk/locker checks and have a certificate for neat desks. Check on the children's work within a few minutes of starting a praise appropriate working behaviour.

Encourage clean ups

Set aside a small amount of time for children to regularly clean out their desks/lockers. Model cleaning behaviour for the children. Ask parents to help their children clean out their bags at the end of each week.

CHAPTER 6 ■ SPECIFIC BEHAVIOUR PROBLEMS—USING THE TEACHER TIP SHEETS

Teach the child to use a diary

Have the child use a daily diary. The child should be taught to write down all the things he needs to remember in the diary. This should include sections for each day titled 'homework', 'things I need to bring to school', 'things I need to tell my parent/s'.

The child should be taught how to break big assignments down into smaller sections and to set personal deadlines for each of the sections (to ensure the child works progressively, rather than the night before it is due).

Have the child's parent/s sign the diary each night to ensure they are also monitoring the child's organisational skills.

When a child is disorganised during class time

Prompt the child

Remind the child to look at the list of instructions and get back on track. Tell the child once what is expected and have him/her repeat the instructions.

Once the child is organised, provide plenty of feedback (specific praise).

Praise organised behaviour in the child and in other children.

Continued disorganisation: consequence

If you need to remind the child more than once to be organised, provide a consequence for the disorganised behaviour. This may involve staying in to finish work, tidying his/her desk, picking up papers during lunch, and so forth.

Provide rewards for completion of work

Allow children who finish their work to have access to a desired activity. The disorganised child may soon learn that there is no benefit in taking longer to complete work because access to fun activities is lost.

Rewards need to be based on quality and not just speed of completion, as some children may rush through their work.

Key steps

- Let children know in advance what they will be doing.
- Colour code books.
- Make a list of instructions.
- Have child repeat the instructions.
- Encourage organised behaviour.
- Teach the child to use a diary.
- Have spot checks and regular clean outs.
- Give rewards for completion of work.

73

74

Parental involvement in behaviour management

7

CHAPTER

Parents are an important factor when managing children's behaviour problems, as they can often provide invaluable support for behaviour change. However, it can be difficult to engage parents initially for a number of reasons. Some parents may perceive that their child's behaviour in the classroom is solely the responsibility of the teacher. Others may be reluctant to become involved because their own management of the child is lacking, or because of other stressors at home. Finally, some parents may have markedly different expectations about behaviour and may not identify the child's behaviour as being in need of change.

The majority of parents, however, are interested in and motivated to assist teachers in improving their child's behaviour. This is particularly true when the focus is on improving skills and behaviour, rather than on punishment of inappropriate behaviour. More reluctant parents can also change their perspective with some encouragement and practical assistance. Some teachers find involving parents in behaviour management a very challenging task which can be made more daunting if the parents are difficult to approach or engage.

While many children with behavioural problems limit their behaviours to only home or only school, there are a smaller number (about 5%) of children who show their inappropriate behaviours across home and school (Little, Hudson & Wilks 2000). For these children, there is a greater likelihood of getting behaviours to change and appropriate behaviour being taught and maintained if both parents and teachers work together. Even when children only display problem behaviours at school, success is heightened if parents assist in reinforcing and monitoring their child's behaviour.

For teachers, it can be a difficult and sometimes daunting task to engage parents in changing a child's behaviour. This is not surprising given the vast range of theories about the best methods for managing behaviour, the philosophies underpinning teaching, and levels of teaching experience. The strategies that will be provided in this chapter are based on principles of applied behaviour analysis, but more importantly they are strategies that work!

Engage parents from the beginning of the year

From the first school day you can provide parents with the opportunity to be involved in the development of appropriate child behaviour. One of the ways to do this is to provide a letter to all parents that outlines the rules of your classroom (that have been jointly formed with your students) and informs them that you will let parents know when a child has been doing the right things (see next page).

This letter also provides you with a chance to shape each parent's behaviour. You can ask them to talk to their child about the what is expected at school and to support letters home with appropriate consequences (praise for good behaviour etc.). You can also invite them to contact you if they have any concerns, making it clear that to do this they will need to arrange an appointment. This is useful information to provide parents, as it will discourage or even prevent them turning up unannounced and expecting you to attend to their concern immediately. Much like any other professional parents need to know that teachers are not entirely flexible in their time. In addition it will allow you time to prepare for the appointment and be ready with information and suggestions for the parents.

Provide feedback for appropriate behaviour

For most people the negative feedback we receive generally outweighs the positive. That is, people tell us when we are doing a bad job but often forget to tell us when we are doing something that is good. This is often the case with children's behaviour. Parents appreciate finding out when their child is doing well and behaving appropriately at school. This is particularly true for parents who have children who do not often behave well in school. They may be very used to receiving letters and phone calls from the school to inform them of all the inappropriate things their child has been doing. It is encouraging both for parents and children to know that the teacher is watching out for appropriate behaviour as well.

Having a letter that you can send home to reinforce a child's appropriate behaviour is a simple way of providing multiple messages. Firstly, it tells the child that his/her good behaviour does not go unnoticed. Secondly, it provides parents with an opportunity to hear something positive about their child. Thirdly, it can act as an additional reinforcement for your classroom behaviour program as you can ask parents to talk to their child about how

Welcome to our classroom

Dear Parent,

Firstly, welcome to the new year and to your child's new classroom. I am keen for you to be kept informed and involved in your child's school life.

We have developed some classroom rules that we are going to use for this year. The rules are:

1. _____

2. _____

3. _____

4. _____

5. _____

Throughout the year I will be sending home letters when children follow the rules and show good behaviour. I hope that you will help me in rewarding these good behaviours.

Your child has been taught the class rules in school, however it would be appreciated if you could also go through them with your child at home.

I am happy to speak with you about any concerns you have about your child. If you would like to see me, please phone to make an appointment as I like to make sure I can talk to parents at a time that allows me to focus fully on your concerns.

Regards,

CHAPTER 7 ▪ PARENTAL INVOLVEMENT IN BEHAVIOUR MANAGEMENT

well they have done at school and what was the desired behaviour. Finally, it will increase the likelihood that parents will assist you when you need their involvement in changing an inappropriate behaviour. A sample letter is provided below.

Good News!

Date:

Dear _____

Just a short note to let you know how pleased I was with _____ **behaviour today.**

I was very pleased with the way your child:

1. _____

2. _____

3. _____

Regards,

Providing feedback for inappropriate behaviour

Once you have established a routine of writing letters home to parents about their child's appropriate behaviour, it then becomes easier to provide feedback about inappropriate behaviour. Parents are aware of what is expected in the classroom and know that their child's good behaviour does not go unnoticed. When you let them know about inappropriate behaviour, you can also focus on what you expect from the child in future.

When informing a parent of inappropriate behaviour, this should be done only if the child is not responding to other classroom-based consequences (such as those discussed earlier). A letter home to parents would be high in the hierarchy of consequences for inappropriate behaviours. Also, you need to consider whether the parent has appropriate skills to support the letter with a consequence at home. At the very least a letter home ensures the parents are aware of their child's behaviour. For parents who are interested and involved, it allows them to reinforce what you are trying to achieve in your classroom with their child.

The letter should provide parents with specific examples of the behaviour and a request that they discuss this with their child (see sample letter structure on the next page).

Some parents may need specific information about why it is important that they become involved in their child's school behaviour. I might write something like:

'Dear Mr and Mrs Smith. We have been working on playing nicely with the other children in the classroom. Unfortunately, James has been having some difficulty with this and three times this week he has been caught hitting other children in the playground at lunchtime. James has been given five minutes of time-out after each occasion, however I am concerned that he has continued to hit other children. In order for James to understand the seriousness of hurting others I would appreciate it if you could discuss this with James. If this behaviour continues, we will need to meet to discuss how we are going to solve this problem.'

It is often a good idea to ask parents to return the letter with their signature on it to ensure the letter is delivered!

CHAPTER 7 ▓ PARENTAL INVOLVEMENT IN BEHAVIOUR MANAGEMENT

School behaviour update

Date:

Dear _____

Just a short note to let you know that _____ **had trouble with his/her behaviour today.**

Today

_____

_____

I have spoken to _____ **and we have agreed that**

_____

If you would like to discuss this with me, please phone to make an appointment.

Regards,

Parent/teacher conference

Parent/teacher conferences can cause a great deal of anxiety both for parents and teachers. When teachers initiate a conference, the anxiety may be caused by concern about how the parent will react to the information about their child.

Another form of stress for teachers occurs when parents initiate a conference. Often this is because teachers are caught off guard by parents (approaching them after school, outside of school, or generally when there has not been a scheduled meeting). When a parent does this, it is useful to acknowledge their concerns and briefly listen to the issue and then make a time for an interview within the next few days. Do not feel compelled to spend time discussing the issue immediately on approach by the parent (unless of course it is something urgent), as you can tell the parent that you would prefer to make a time when you are free of distractions and able to focus on their specific concerns.

For interviews that are occurring outside the usual twice yearly parent/teacher interviews, it is useful to tell your principal about the meeting. This ensures that you have ready support if you need it, and allows the principal to be forewarned in the unlikely instance of the parent also confronting him/her.

Before the interview take time to write down notes about the child (both positive and negative) and think about the child across a range of areas: academic, behavioural; and social. You might want to write down a list of issues that you need to cover with the parent/s. It is helpful to have these specific bits of information as it then allows you to separate the child's behaviour from the child and gives you manageable areas to work on.

On the following page is a proforma of a parent/teacher conference form. You can document your concerns, the parents' response and the joint decisions on it. As a teacher, it is always a good idea to keep written records of your meetings with parents and decisions made in these meetings.

CHAPTER 7 ▪ PARENTAL INVOLVEMENT IN BEHAVIOUR MANAGEMENT

Parent/teacher conference

Child's name: _____   **Date:** _____

Teacher concerns:	
Parent concerns/ response	
Outcomes/action— teacher	
Outcomes/action— parent	
Outcomes/action— child	

Signed _____ (parent)   _____ (teacher)

83

It is also a good idea to have at least three positives to report to the parents before you bring up any negatives. Firstly, this hopefully will get the parents on side as they understand that you do notice when their child does something good. Also, it prevents parents becoming immediately defensive of themselves and their child, so they are more likely to listen. Finally, it reduces some of the stress of having to discuss behaviour problems, as you start off on a positive note.

Provide the parent with specific examples, work samples, information that you have recorded and so on, so that you have concrete examples of the concerns. This will enhance your own credibility and provide parents with the opportunity to get a very clear picture of what is happening with their child.

Research has demonstrated that many children do not show the same behaviours at home as they do at school (Little, Hudson & Wilks 2000), and it is worth keeping this in mind if parents challenge statements that you make about their child. It is useful to use phrases such as 'when Jarryd is at school he . . .' Or 'I'm wondering if Blake does this at home, because it certainly is a problem at school'. If the parent claims that the child does not behave the same way at home, you could perhaps use this to highlight the differences across the two settings that might lead to the problems.

It is also useful to provide the parent with an opportunity to reflect on what is happening at home. Are there any major changes? What does the child report about school? What things does the parent do at home with the child? This gives you information about how much the parent can be involved in any strategies you decide to take to change the inappropriate behaviour.

During your conference with the parent, try to come up with some possible solutions to the problems and write these down. This allows you to ensure there is a common understanding of the problem and the goals and strategies that are to be used. If possible, both you and the parent/s should take on a task so that there is dual responsibility.

Finally, if a parent becomes angry, aggressive or abusive then it is clear that trying to get them to see your perspective is not working. Try to diffuse their anger by acknowledging it and suggesting that you should give them some time to think about your concerns and meet again at a later date. It is not useful to get into a heated discussion with a parent and may put you in a vulnerable position. If all else fails, excuse yourself and get a colleague to come in for the remainder of the interview.

Targeting specific groups

8

CHAPTER

Teachers know better than anyone that there are many things outside of their control that can impact on what happens in the classroom. These can include the nature and personality of the children they teach, family circumstances of their students, personal events for the teachers and many other factors. In the next two chapters I will cover some of the more topical issues that are impacting on the classroom. Firstly, we will look at Attention Deficit Hyperactivity Disorder and the impact this has on the child and the classroom. Then we will look at the issue of parental separation and divorce and what teachers can do to help a child deal with these situations. This will be followed by a discussion of the specific needs of those in the middle years of schooling.

Attention Deficit Hyperactivity Disorder (ADHD)

Attention Deficit Hyperactivity Disorder (ADHD) is currently receiving a lot of media attention, however what this term means is often not well understood. Are children with ADHD just naughty children? Are they children whose parents can't control them? Is there really such a condition as ADHD at all?

ADHD is a real disorder with very real consequences for children socially, emotionally, behaviourally and academically. The title ADHD comes from the American Psychiatric Association's Diagnostic and Statistical Manual for Mental Disorders—volume 4 (APA, 1994). The symptoms of ADHD have been noted in children for centuries; it is not a new disorder. The behaviours identified included impulsive, inattentive and hyperactive behaviours. Over the years, this combination of symptoms has been given many different labels.

Currently the term used is Attention Deficit Hyperactivity Disorder. ADHD is diagnosed using a symptom checklist developed by the American Psychiatric Association. This is a world wide standard for diagnosis and the criteria for ADHD were developed by a team of experts in the area of child behaviour using the available research in an attempt to describe the features of this disorder and associated characteristics.

Currently three types of ADHD are identified: (1) ADHD predominantly inattentive type; (2) ADHD predominantly Hyperactive-impulsive type; and (3) ADHD combined type. In the box on the next page are the criteria used to determine a diagnosis of ADHD.

CHAPTER 8 ■ TARGETING SPECIFIC GROUPS

Diagnostic criteria (DSM-IV: APA, 1994)

A. Either (1) or (2)

1. Six (or more) of the following symptoms of inattention have persisted for at least 6 months to a degree that is maladaptive and inconsistent with developmental level.

Inattention

a. often fails to give close attention to details or makes careless mistakes in schoolwork, work, or other activities

b. often has difficulty sustaining attention in tasks or play activities

c. often does not seem to listen when spoken to directly

d. often does not follow through on instructions and fails to finish schoolwork, chores, or duties in the workplace (not due to oppositional behaviour or failure to understand instructions)

e. often has difficulty organizing tasks and activities

f. often avoids, dislikes, or is reluctant to engage in tasks that require sustained mental effort (such as school work/homework)

g. often loses things necessary for tasks or activities (e.g. toys, assignments, pencils, books, or tools)

h. is often easily distracted by extraneous stimuli

i. is often forgetful in daily activities.

2. Six (or more) of the following symptoms of hyperactivity-impulsivity have persisted for at least six months to a degree that is maladaptive and inconsistent with developmental level.

Hyperactivity

a. often fidgets with hands or feet or squirms in seat

b. often leaves seat in classroom or in other situations in which remaining seated is expected

c. often runs about or climbs excessively in situations in which it is inappropriate (in adolescents or adults, may be limited to subjective feelings of restlessness)

d. often has difficulty playing or engaging in leisure activities quietly

e. is often 'on the go' or often acts as if 'driven by a motor'

f. often talks excessively.

Impulsivity

a. often blurts out answers before questions are completed

b. often has difficulty awaiting turn

c. often interrupts or intrudes on others (e.g. butts into conversations or games)

B. Some hyperactive-impulsive symptoms that caused impairment were present before age 7 years.

> **C.** Some impairment from the symptoms is present in two or more settings (e.g. at school [or work] and at home)
>
> **D.** There must be clear evidence of clinically significant impairment in social, academic, or occupational functioning.
>
> **E.** The symptoms do not occur exclusively during the course of a pervasive developmental disorder, schizophrenia, or other psychotic disorder, and are not better accounted for by another mental disorder (e.g. mood disorder, anxiety disorder, dissociative disorder, personality disorder).
>
> **Code based on type:**
>
> **314.01 Attention-Deficit/Hyperactivity Disorder, Combined type:** if both Criteria A1 and A2 are met for the past 6 months.
>
> **314.00 Attention-Deficit/Hyperactivity Disorder, Predominantly Inattentive type:** if Criterion A1 is met but not A2.
>
> **314.01 Attention-Deficit/Hyperactivity Disorder, Predominantly Hyperactive-Impulsive type:** if Criterion A2 is met but A1 is not.

Reprinted with permission from the *Diagnostic and Statistical Manual of Mental Disorders, Text Revision*, Copyright 2000 American Psychiatric Association.

As a summary of the above features, you are likely to see a child who has a number of behaviours that involve a lack of impulse control (impulsivity), being constantly on the move, or difficulty maintaining attention. As you are well aware, every child will demonstrate these behaviours sometimes. The child with ADHD displays many of these behaviours, most of the time.

Across settings

It is very important to note that clinicians should only diagnose ADHD if the behaviours are seen across more than one setting (for example home and school). This theoretically should rule out a child who is simply misbehaving because his parents are not controlling him/her. ADHD can be incorrectly diagnosed if information isn't obtained from a range of sources. This is why a teacher's involvement in the diagnosis is extremely important.

Who makes the diagnosis?

A diagnosis of ADHD should only be made by someone who is an expert in child behaviour. People such as psychologists, psychiatrists, pediatricians and some medical practitioners who have a thorough understanding of developmental psychology and child psychopathology are generally in the best position to make an informed diagnosis. Before

CHAPTER 8 ▪ TARGETING SPECIFIC GROUPS

diagnosing ADHD the practitioner should conduct a thorough investigation of the child's behaviour. This generally will include standardised testing of the child; use of ADHD symptom checklists with parents and teachers; observation of the child (preferably outside of a clinic setting) and careful consideration of any other possible causes of the child's behaviour (stressful life event, illness, environment and so forth). Using such a rigorous procedure should greatly reduce the likelihood of a child being diagnosed incorrectly.

Unfortunately, there are some children whose diagnosis of ADHD may not have been made with the aforementioned procedure. It is fair to say that there may be some children diagnosed with ADHD, who don't meet the criteria set out by the APA. However, it is important to point out that the bulk of research in the area does agree that ADHD is a real disorder that has impacts on the child and those around him.

Who has ADHD?

Around 3 to 5% of children have ADHD (APA 1994). This means than in an average class it is likely that one child would meet the criteria for ADHD. Three times as many boys as girls have ADHD in the general population. However, when we look at referrals to clinic settings (psychologists, psychiatrists, inpatient) boys are referred six times more often than girls. In a recent survey 83% of current teachers had taught at least one child with ADHD in their teaching career (Kos, Richdale & Jackson 2002). Most teachers had taught more than one child with ADHD. Therefore, it is something that you will be dealing with in your classroom at some stage.

What are the impacts of ADHD?

Like any disruptive behaviour ADHD impacts on the child, parents, teacher and peers. Children with ADHD are often isolated from their peers because of their impulsive and inattentive behaviours. Other children may not be tolerant of a child who is constantly on the move, or who has difficulty waiting turn, or who has difficulty maintaining attention.

Children with ADHD are more likely than their peers to have learning difficulties. One study demonstrated that between 15 and 38 per cent of children with ADHD have reading difficulties, compared to up to 8 per cent of children without ADHD (Semrud-Clikemen et al. 1992). Therefore, it is often necessary to also address these learning difficulties and provide a structured individual approach to teaching the child.

89

The child with ADHD may perceive himself/herself as different from other children and may be embarrassed by his/her own behaviour. One boy that I worked with had a great deal of difficulty in complying with his medication routine. When I talked to him about this he admitted that the reason he often didn't take his medication during the day was because he had to go to the principal to ask for it and was embarrassed. Given that an adult generally should be the one to provide the medication, it is worth talking to the parents about how best to manage this to reduce any compliance issues. It may be possible for the child to be involved in deciding who will oversee his medication at school.

How is ADHD treated?

In Australia, the National Health and Medical Research Council recommends that multiple management strategies be used to treat ADHD (NHMRC 1997). Generally this could involve behaviour management, medication, family intervention and educational intervention. Because a child with ADHD does not just have difficulties with the symptoms in only one setting, it is also recommended that both parents and teachers be involved in the management of the child's difficulties.

By far the most well known treatment for ADHD involves the use of medication, generally involving psychostimulants. The two most common of these stimulant medications are Methylphenidate (Ritalin) and Dextroamphetamine. It seems strange to most people that we give stimulants to kids who are already hyperactive—wouldn't they just become more hyperactive? It is important to understand that stimulants are named not for the effect that they have on behaviour, but rather because they stimulate central nervous system functioning. These neurotransmitters are involved in regulating attention, impulse control, memory, behavioural inhibition and executive functioning (NHMRC 1997). Therefore, they have an effect on the behaviours that are generally problematic for children with ADHD. There is a great deal of debate in the literature about the effectiveness and safety of using stimulant medications to manage ADHD. However, much of the recent research indicates that when medication is given appropriately (that is to children who actually have ADHD) and is closely monitored, it is effective in reducing the negative symptoms of ADHD (for a review of the evidence see NHMRC 1997).

The effects of medication that are generally seen in the classroom include improved on-task behaviour, increased performance on academic tasks and increased work output, reduced aggression and antisocial behaviours, and increased appropriate social

CHAPTER 8 ■ TARGETING SPECIFIC GROUPS

interactions (see NHMRC 1997 for more detailed review). In summary, medications have been demonstrated to be effective and these effects are noticed by others. Side effects that have been reported include appetite suppression, sleep disturbance, changes in mood and headaches (Barkley et al. 1990). Often these side effects can be reduced through careful manipulation of dosage and timing of medication.

While medication is commonly used to treat ADHD, there are also alternative strategies to manage ADHD that can be used alone or in addition to stimulants. Behaviour management strategies can be used both at home and in the school setting with children with ADHD. Educational and developmental psychologists often work in conjunction with medical practitioners in providing parent training programs alongside medication. Such programs typically use the same strategies that have been mentioned in this book for use in the home setting (e.g. Sanders & Dadds 1993).

What can teachers do to help children with ADHD?

Diagnosis

One of the primary ways that teachers can help is in identification. You may be asked to provide information to the diagnosing clinician—this may take the form of a questionnaire, interview or even providing access for observation of the child by the clinician. You may also be the person who first notices that the child is exhibiting the symptoms of ADHD. Using the diagnostic criteria listed earlier you are in a good position to determine whether the child is behaving in a way that is consistent with a diagnosis. If the child is, then it may be useful to speak with the parents about the specific behaviours of concern and perhaps suggest that a more thorough investigation is conducted by your school psychologist (or a clinician of the parents' choice).

Management

All of the strategies that have been mentioned throughout this book can be applied for children with ADHD. For example, a child who has difficulty staying on task can be assisted by the strategies listed in the tip sheet. Using reinforcement for appropriate behaviours and consequences for inappropriate behaviours can assist a child in learning to develop self control skills. I am not suggesting that ADHD is really just a child being 'naughty', but rather children with ADHD may need to be explicitly taught the attentional skills and strategies to control impulses that other children may have learnt incidentally.

In addition, these types of strategies work very well alongside medication. Often the medication reduces the child's inattentive, hyperactive or impulsive behaviours enough that the behavioural strategies can be taught. However, as pointed out earlier compliance to medication may be an issue for some children. Also, given that most children have two doses during the day it is likely that the school will be asked to administer the second dose. This needs to be carefully discussed with the parents, principal and school nurse (if applicable) to determine the extent of responsibility the school is willing to take and to consider potential problems with compliance. It is strongly recommended that the child not take containers of medication to school himself as there are risks of both the child and other children misusing this medication.

Other suggestions include:

- having more breaks in academic learning time. Rather than have the child try to focus for an hour (which may not be manageable), set on-task time to 20 or 30 minutes and then give the child a couple of minutes' break before starting again. This is likely to lead to less disruptive behaviour as the child has shorter goals (in terms of time) to work towards.

- Using visual aids to keep the child on task (e.g. using a timer or clock to indicate the time expected for the child to be on task). Provide lists of tasks on the board so the child doesn't have to ask what he or she is supposed to be doing.

- Breaking assignments into manageable parts—have the child work on one part at a time. This is less overwhelming than trying to tackle the whole piece at once.

- Keeping the momentum going in class—interest will be maintained if there is little 'down time'.

Divorce and separation

It is an unfortunate reality that many children are going to experience parental separation and divorce. Given the ever-increasing divorce rate, 1 in 3 children is likely to experience a divorce within the family before the age of 18 (Australian Bureau of Statistics 2002). For these children school may be their only stable environment and a place where they feel secure and comfortable. Alternatively, school may become the outlet for their emotional distress and their behaviour and academic performance may reflect this. How should teachers handle these situations? Should you talk to the child about what's going on?

One teacher that I know faced this situation with a boy in his class. The boy's parents had recently separated and there was a high level of conflict between them. The boy's mum had told the teacher that she and her husband had separated and said that she was worried about how her son might react at school. The teacher decided to speak to the child quietly after school one day and simply said to him, 'I know things are a bit rough at home at the moment, if you want to talk about it to me you can. But, if you want to try to forget about it when you are at school then that is okay too'. This particular child wanted to forget about it when he was at school and on the occasions when he felt a bit upset he was allowed to take some time out to compose himself. For this child, not being treated differently was very important.

Some parents will not tell you about what is happening at home, and you may be left trying to work out why a child's behaviour and academic performance has suddenly changed. A situation such as this may become tricky because you then may be approaching parents who themselves are under a great deal of stress and very fragile. Later in this section I will give you some ideas on how to approach this issue with parents.

Effect of divorce on children

Children who are in divorced or remarried families have been found to have lower self-esteem, increased problematic behaviour and academic problems and more difficulties interacting with others, than children from nondivorced families (Hetherington, Bridges & Insabella 1998). However, these effects are not always seen in all children and can depend a great deal on the specifics of the situation. For example, children from families where there was a great deal of conflict before parental separation and a low level of conflict following separation often experience fewer negative effects than those in families that don't break up but are high in conflict. Conflict between parents seems to be a critical element in the effects of divorce on children. When there is high conflict, parents have difficulty communicating and this may prevent them effectively co-parenting (Shifflett & Cummings 1999) and may lead to the use of the child as a mediator.

Generally children who experience divorce initially experience a great deal of sadness and grief about their parents' separation. They will often spend a lot of time wishing that their parents would reconcile and trying to work out how they might be able to help that happen. Often children blame themselves for the separation and may latch on to certain behaviours as explanations for their parents' separation. Children may have many fears about what will happen to them, where they will live, whether they will see their noncustodial parent, and whether their parents still love them. After all, in the eyes of a child, if you can stop loving another adult, then you might be able to stop loving a child. Often these are fears that need to be addressed by the parents. However, as the teacher and a trusted adult you may be faced with children looking to you for reassurance.

It is also important to point out that the effects of divorce may depend on the child's age, their gender, and the nature of the separation. In a review of the literature, Richardson and Rosen (1999) report that children aged 6 to 8 have a limited understanding of divorce. Children in the early years of school are likely to feel sadness and anger about the separation. Aggression, separation anxiety and tantrums are common behaviours seen in this age group following separation or divorce (Hodges 1986). It is also common for children of this age to perceive that they might be responsible for the separation, as discussed earlier. For example, a young child might think his parent left because he/she never kept his room clean.

Children aged 9 to 12 have a greater ability to understand divorce and while they might have many of the same reactions to divorce as younger children, according to Cantrell (1996; as cited in Richardson & Rosen 1999) at this age they are more likely to be intensely angry. This anger is often directed at the parents, and more often than not it is toward one parent whom they particularly believe is responsible for the separation.

Divorce and school

It is likely that the child who is experiencing parental separation will demonstrate behaviour changes at school. Often the child can feel extremely anxious about whether other important adults in their life may also leave. Children who are given emotional support in the school setting have been found to exhibit fewer of the negative symptoms found with divorce (Stolberg & Mahler 1994). With this support, the anxiety, worry and general difficulties following divorce have found to be reduced (Cowen, Pedro-Carroll & Alpert-Gillis 1990).

Some ideas about what you can do in the classroom

Ask questions

This might mean asking the child how he or she is going if you are aware that there has been a separation or divorce. I think it is a good idea to ask the child if there is anything that might help him/her at school. One thing that a child might welcome could be the opportunity to take a bit of time out if they feel too sad (this could be as simple as going and sitting in the reading area for a few minutes). A child might also want to know who they can talk to if they need to. I think teachers themselves should avoid becoming too involved in talking with the child as this may lead to you being seen as some sort of counsellor, however you could talk to them about seeing the Student Welfare Coordinator or school psychologist (if available) or someone external to the school.

If the child's behaviour has changed or if you believe something is worrying the child you may also need to ask the child's parents what is happening. In my experience it is often the case that other people may tell you that there has been a parental separation. For example, parents of other children or even other teachers may have found this information out and pass it on to you. In this case, you may want to clarify what is happening. I believe that it is important to do this as you can then more thoroughly understand the child's behaviour and be able to make allowances or address the situation as required.

Just as in any situation involving approaching parents you need to consider how you are going to raise your concerns. Perhaps you could start off by saying, '*James does not seem to have been himself lately. He has been a bit teary at school and has been having difficulty doing work that he usually is able to manage. Do you have any ideas about why this might be the case?*' Using this type of questioning is less accusational for parents than 'is there something happening at home?' and provides the parent with an opportunity to understand that the child's unhappiness is being noticed and is affecting him at school.

If a parent discloses a separation to you, then it is useful to acknowledge the distress this must be causing. For example, 'I am very sorry to hear that, this must be a very difficult time for the whole family'. Again, you are acknowledging that it is okay for there to be some disturbance to the whole family's functioning. I would then follow on with, 'is there anything that we can do for James at school to help him out? Perhaps we could refer him to see the student welfare coordinator?'

It is also useful to find out practically what this means for the child. For example, is the child living in the same place? Will he/she be alternating residences? Are both parents going to be involved in the decision making for the child? Will the child be able to do homework? While you want to avoid being too probing, it is important to point out to the parent that all of these things will influence the child's functioning at school.

Divorce can also mean changes in legal guardianship and custody arrangements. This can become a minefield for teachers!!! You need to ensure that the appropriate parent/s provide consent for their child to undertake activities, that reports get sent to the right place, that a parent does have the right to collect his/her child from school and so forth. It is important that the school records are current and accurate to ensure that you are doing the right thing for the child.

Provide normality

Given that the child's home environment might be unpredictable and confusing for the child, it is important that his/her life at school remains relatively consistent, predictable and stable. Therefore, while it is important to know the child's situation it is also important that the child does not suddenly find that he/she is being treated differently at school. The routine of the day, his/her friends, and relationship with you are all things that will provide a sense of normality. If he/she misbehaves, provide the same sorts of consequences as you would before. If the child's behaviour changes dramatically then I would immediately speak with the parents and refer on to the school psychologist or other clinicians (counsellor, psychologist, psychiatrist etc.).

Make some allowances

This may now sound like a contradiction, but while you want the classroom experience to remain relatively stable for the child you also need to make some adjustments to the expectations you have for the child. Doing homework at home may be difficult if there is a lot of conflict or distress, or if the child is trying to deal with his/her own emotions and is having difficulty concentrating. Perhaps homework tasks could be reduced or the child could be provided with some time during the school day to do some homework. Concentrating on school work generally may be affected and you may need to adjust the work the child has to complete and the amount of time he/she can do it in.

Link the child to support

Some schools or school regions might provide support groups for children from divorced or separated families. Such groups are extremely useful in helping children communicate their feelings, work on their perception of themselves (e.g. often children blame themselves for parental separation), teach them problem solving and anger management techniques and possibly most importantly link them in with other children who understand what they are going through. Even if it is just getting children who have experienced divorce together and providing them with an outlet for emotions and emotional support, this greatly improves their chances of adjusting adaptively to the separation.

Some researchers suggest that group therapy is the most effective method of helping children from divorced families (Guldner & O'Connor 1991). This is based on the notion that group programs reduce isolation, increase normality and provide peer support (Gladding 1991). If your school has the opportunity to develop a group program for children from divorced families, DeLucia-Waack and Gerrity (2001) provide directions as to the content and structure of such an intervention.

American psychologists developed a program that can be run in schools as a preventative intervention for children of divorce called 'the children of divorce intervention program' or CODIP. This targets primary school children and works to develop group support and social and coping skills. Following the program children were found to have increased academic competencies, and decreased behaviour problems both at home and at school (Pedro-Carroll & Cowen 1985). The program generally runs over 12 sessions and has been used with children aged five right through to late primary school. Children aged five and six were followed up two years after the program and were found to have less anxiety, fewer classroom problems and visits to the school nurse compared to children not in the program (Pedro-Carroll, Sutton & Wyman 1999). While it is not practical for teachers themselves to run such a program in the classroom, there are some important elements that can be incorporated into the school environment to assist children going through parental separation and divorce. In addition you may be able to speak with the school principal, student welfare coordinator or school psychologist about the possibility of organising a group for children from separated or divorced families.

Summary

It is important to remember that parental separation does not always lead to divorce and that some families will end up reconciled. So for some children the separation of parents may be a short-term situation. However, the initial response from the child will be the same as for those children whose parents end up divorcing. The difference in child reaction lies in how they respond when the parents reconcile. For many children, while this may be a happy event, there may also be ongoing issues that warrant attention. Fear that the parents will again separate usually tops the list. The child may be very anxious to please both parents and cause as little trouble as possible in the belief that this will keep them together. The child could also feel a great deal of anger towards his parents for separating in the first place and may demonstrate this through acting out behaviours. In any case, reconciliation can also cause a great deal of stress for the child and may warrant referral to an appropriate agency.

Divorce in families is increasing in prevalence and it is an unfortunate reality that more and more of your students will have to deal with parental separation. It is a good idea to try to set up a support structure within your school to ensure that there are consistent and effective strategies to help children from newly separated (as well as divorced) families.

Middle years of schooling

Another area that has been receiving a great deal of recent attention is the middle years of schooling. This covers children from Year 6 to Year 9 and recognises that during these years there are issues that need to be considered. Across these years children are affected by a number of transitions that can have a negative effect on their functioning. This includes the transition from primary to secondary school and the transition from childhood to adolescence.

The physical, emotional and social changes that occur during the middle years can be extremely stressful for children and young adolescents. Those who do not have adequate coping skills or support may become disengaged and suffer from a myriad of difficulties. While the majority of adolescents cope successfully with these changes and move into adulthood as competent and confident people, there are those who will struggle. A key challenge across these years is to develop resiliency, which is 'the happy knack of being ably to bungy jump through the pitfalls of life' (Fuller 1998, p. 75). A key feature of building

CHAPTER 8 ■ TARGETING SPECIFIC GROUPS

resiliency is having one stable, supportive and uncritical adult involved throughout this period (Fuller 1998). This is often a parent, but for children whose family lives are not stable or supportive then schools may need to play a more significant role in developing these connections.

For those teachers who have a lot to do with adolescents, Andrew Fuller's book *From Surviving to Thriving* (1988) is a must-have text. He provides a whole range of strategies that can be used by parents, teachers and other adults to help adolescents. In the following sections we will briefly look at some of the issues for students in the middle years of schooling.

Social and emotional changes

As children move into adolescence they experience many changes. Puberty can be a traumatic time as children change physically and emotionally (remember those hormones!). Most schools now provide many opportunities for students to learn about growth and development that are far removed from the 'Sex Ed' of years ago. Rather, children are now exposed to life education that covers physical and emotional development, families, and social issues (e.g. drugs, peer group pressure). Educating children about these physical, emotional and social changes makes them easier to accept and less frightening. If it does not go against your school or state policy, it is a good idea to ensure that your students are provided with this education. Often these classes are taken by external agencies, with the teacher sitting in with the children rather than conducting the lessons. You may not feel comfortable in talking about these issues with your class (and who could blame you?). However, being there demonstrates to the class that this is important and provides them with someone else to ask questions of if needed.

When you are teaching in the middle years, you notice that children start to change physically. The children notice this as well, and this can cause social difficulties. Consider the child who is an early developer. He or she suddenly looks different to his/her peers and may be experiencing a whole lot of physical changes that seem to be abnormal because no one else is going through them. Given that people in general pay a lot of attention to physical characteristics, this can also lead to unwanted attention in the form of teasing.

The middle years sees an higher level of teasing and bullying that tapers as students move into the upper years of schooling (Nansel et al. 2001). Therefore, social relationships can be particularly an issue for the middle years. During this period friendships often change, peer pressure becomes more noticeable, and the young adolescent may more frequently compare themselves to others. Generally children want to fit in and be like everyone else. Bullying is an important issue for both primary and secondary schools as research indicates that around 18–27% of students in the middle years are victims of frequent bullying (Borg 1999). Therefore, a whole-school approach to the prevention and intervention of bullying should be taken. Ken Rigby's book *Bullying in schools and what to do about it* is a valuable source of information for teachers, administrators and parents.

In addition to the peer conflict that may become more prevalent in the middle years, parents and children start spending more time in conflict and children may no longer see conforming with adults' expectations as desirable. Praise in public (that works so well for younger students) may suddenly become something that is avoided at all costs! In a recent survey of secondary school students the overwhelming majority reported that public praise was not something that would be reinforcing and in fact could be seen as punishment (Infantino & Little, 2002). Therefore, classroom management strategies may need to be reconsidered to ensure you are using rewards that students actually want.

A range of psychological difficulties may also become more noticeable in the middle years. Adolescence is a peak time for depression, self-harm, and eating disorders to appear. These can often be difficult to detect and typically require referral to a mental health clinician. If you notice a change in a student's mood, work productivity and quality, appearance (e.g. rapid weight gain or loss, change in personal hygiene, unexplained marks on body) then it may be worthwhile approaching the student or the student's parents with your concerns. Given that adolescents often find it difficult to disclose their personal problems, you may find that the adolescent denies there is a problem. In most cases discussing your concerns with the student's parents is appropriate. If this is not possible, then talk to the year level coordinator or student welfare coordinator about your concerns.

Educational difficulties

I have noticed that around Year 4 to 5 seems to be a time when some children markedly struggle academically. It is often at this point that Educational Psychologists have a larger number of referrals for academic assessments and intervention. It seems that for some students this is the time that their learning difficulties become most obvious and more overwhelming.

CHAPTER 8 ■ TARGETING SPECIFIC GROUPS

It may be the case that as students enter the middle years of schooling, the academic tasks that they undertake become more heavily based on complex literacy skills (even numeracy tasks become more language based). The amount and level of literacy activities increases and students who may have been a bit behind their peers, start to lag even further behind as their compensatory strategies start to fall apart.

It is not the purpose of this book to discuss instructional approaches to academic tasks, as there is a great deal of literature in this area and there are many different theoretical approaches to teaching areas such as literacy and numeracy. However, for those children who are struggling academically in the middle years it may be worthwhile considering their individual needs for instruction. Speak to your curriculum coordinator about the literacy and numeracy programs that are appropriate for addressing the specific concerns of the individual child (these will differ depending on the difficulties the child is experiencing).

For the child who does appear to be struggling with the academic tasks, it may be useful to make a referral to an educational psychologist. The educational psychologist can conduct an in-depth assessment of the child's cognitive ability and learning style, and determine where the difficulties are arising from. The school psychologist would generally write a thorough psycho-educational report for the parents and school making recommendations about how best to assist the child. This would usually be followed by a meeting with the parents and teacher to develop an individual strategy to assist the child. This often involves the parents as well as the teacher implementing interventions to assist the child.

School transition

The transition from primary to secondary school can be a difficult one for many students. While it may sound clichéd, they do go from being big fish in a little pond, to little fish in a very big pond. The difference between Year 7 students (who are still very much children) and Year 12 students (who are almost adults) is enormous, and very noticeable to the new high school student. Often leaving primary school can be a time of great anxiety and trauma as the child says goodbye to all that has been familiar for seven years. Changing to a new school, with a whole lot of new teachers, unfamiliar buildings, and intimidating older students can lead to the emergence of anxiety, adjustment problems, and even school refusal. It has been demonstrated that transition can impact motivation and academic achievement (Galloway et al. 1998; Sainbury et al. 1998).

101

Teachers can assist in making the transition less stressful for students, particularly Year 6 and Year 7 teachers. This is particularly true when the majority of children are moving from one local school to another. For those children who are going to a different school more individualised transition may need to be considered if the child appears to be at risk of poor adjustment.

Increase familiarity

Gradually introduce the Year 6 students to the high school environment throughout the year. Organising interschool activities is a good way to do this. Have the students go to the high school to watch sporting or drama activities. Get them involved in cross-age programs so that they get to know some familiar faces.

Introduce the school environment

Have the children create their own map of the secondary school they will be going to—this works for all children. Get them to draw in important places, such as the toilets, canteen, library, school nurse and principal's office. Have them work out how far it is from their house, how they will get there, what sort of transport they need to take and so on. These activities can be incorporated into you regular curriculum to make them less obviously related to the move at the end of the year. For example, a maths activity could involve comparing the sizes (area) of the secondary school and the primary school.

Have a buddy program

Team up the Year 6 students with a current Year 7 student. You need to be wary of having 'buddies' who are a lot older (e.g. Year 9 or 10 students) as this might then cause more stress for the younger students. Get them to write letters to each other throughout the year and organise a number of academic activities that they can do together. If possible have the Year 6 students spend a day or half a day with the Year 7 students at secondary school.

Learn the daily structure

The secondary school day is usually quite different to what happens at primary school. Teachers change for each class, students have to move from one place to another, they may use lockers for the first time, and they may have far more classes in one day than they are used to. Therefore it is helpful to spend time looking at a typical secondary school day with the children. The best way to do this would be to have them spend a day before the start of the high school year in the high school. If this isn't possible, then you may be able to create

CHAPTER 8 ■ TARGETING SPECIFIC GROUPS

a high school experience in the primary school. You could invite teachers from the secondary school to come along a run a sample class, restructure the classes for the day, and have them move to the next class instead of staying in their own room.

Communication between teachers and parents

Parents may also be anxious about their child starting school, so a transition program for parents may also be helpful. A joint information evening is often a good way to manage this, with teachers from both schools involved. You can talk about what will be done in the primary school to prepare students, what happens at secondary school, and how the students will be assisted once they move into the new school. This also gives parents an opportunity en masse to ask questions, which may reduce the number of individual meetings you need to organise.

Creating connections

Students are often anxious because their new school teachers don't know who they are. This may be combated by having the children create an introductory booklet about themselves that they can give to their home room teacher at high school. This could either be done at the end of Year 6 or the start of Year 7. Get them to include a photo of themselves, information about their families, their likes and dislikes, and anything else that they think is important. This may also be very helpful to the secondary school teachers who often have multiple classes of Year 7 students, making the job of learning names and faces even more difficult.

104

Looking after yourself

CHAPTER

Teaching is one of the most stressful occupations because of the constant demands placed on teachers, the lack of autonomy and the politics that surround the profession. It is a good idea to monitor how you are coping and make sure you have effective strategies for dealing with stress. Often we can not avoid stress, particularly in a job such as teaching, so this last chapter is devoted to strategies for making sure you stay emotionally well.

Physical health

Look after your physical health and wellbeing. Make sure your diet provides you with adequate sources of energy to make it through your day—do not skip meals. This also means taking time to recover if you are unwell. I know many teachers who will not take time off when they are sick, and this only ends up making the situation worse.

Exercise! Take time out each day to go for a walk or do some form of activity that gets your pulse up a little—you do not have to run or do weights (30 minutes of moderate intensity physical activity a day would be perfect). This can be hard to begin, so try to get someone else to join you. Get up 30 minutes earlier of a morning and go for a walk with your partner, meet another teacher at school before you begin the day, go for a stroll at lunchtime or after school. Physical activity reduces stress, increases physical health and longevity, reduces depression and creates general feelings of wellbeing. It gives you time out from your worries and might even become a social activity.

If you have not exercised before, start off with something simple. Just going for a short walk for 5 minutes is a good place to begin. If you are going to start an actual exercise program, make sure you get a checkup from your doctor first.

Indulge yourself

Schedule some pleasurable activities for yourself—and not just during the school holidays. Have a massage once a month, or go out for coffee after work occasionally, catch up with friends on the weekend, take a long bath, or see a movie. Make sure you have an interest outside of work, as this will give you something pleasant to think about and look forward to.

CHAPTER 9 ■ JUST QUICKLY: TAKING CARE OF YOURSELF

Try to have at least one day of the weekend free of school work (if you can do all your work at school and not bring it home at all, that's even better). When you have 30 children with you five days a week, you will need some time out on the weekends. You also need to spend time with adult friends outside of your workplace. It has been repeatedly demonstrated that people who have good social supports are better able to deal with stress.

Remember that you are not able to be everything to all people and that you are only human. Sometimes you need to say no to demands that are placed on you. It is also okay to ask for help. Rather than trying to deal with your worries and stresses by yourself, it might be useful to talk to someone else about them.

Relaxation

One of the simplest and most effective ways to relax is to use deep, gentle breathing. When we are tense or stressed, one of the first responses of the body is to breathe faster. This leads to all those symptoms of anxiety and stress: muscle tension; increased heart rate; dizziness; digestive problems; increased sweating and so on. Slowing down your breathing can quickly lead to a reduction in anxiety and stress symptoms.

Try this when you are feeling tense or stressed.

Deep breathing

1. Breathe in to the count of three—a deep breath that goes all the way to your stomach 1 … 2 … 3 …

2. Hold the breath for two seconds 1 … 2 …

3. Breathe out to the count of three—pushing the breath out from your stomach all the way up your chest 1 … 2 … 3 …

4. As you breathe out say 'Relax' (in your head)

5. Repeat this four times.

Other ways to relax include learning meditation, progressive muscle relaxation or taking classes in yoga.

The important message to take from this is that you need to be proactive about reducing your stress levels and managing the physical signs and symptoms of stress. If you feel that you are not coping, tell someone (such as a GP, counsellor or friend).

Final word

CHAPTER 10

Teaching is one of the most (if not the most) challenging jobs in the world. You are required to be an educator, a behaviour change agent, a social worker, a mediator, and a role model. It is not surprising that this can be a daunting task, even more so when you have a child (or children) in your class who is behaving in inappropriate ways. Fortunately teaching can also be one of the most rewarding jobs, and in this book I have given you some ideas about how you can turn the challenges into rewards.

References

American Psychiatric Association (1994) *Diagnostic and statistical manual of mental disorders*. 4th ed. Author: Washington, DC.

Australian Bureau of Statistics (2002) *Marriages and Divorces, Australia*. Author: Canberra.

Barkley, RA, McMurray, MB, Edelbrock, CS, Robbins, K (1990) 'Side effects of methylphenidate in children with attention deficit hyperactivity disorder: a systemic, placebo controlled evaluation'. *Pediatrics*, *86*, 184–92.

Bell, ML & Davidson, CW (1976) 'Relationships between pupil-on-task performance and pupil achievement'. *The Journal of Educational Research*, *69*, 172–76.

Borg, M (1999) 'The extent and nature of bullying among primary and secondary schoolchildren'. *Educational Research*, *41*, 137–53.

Brophy, JE (1982) 'Classroom management and learning'. *American Education*, *March*, 20–3.

Canter, L & Canter, M (1976, 1982) *Assertive discipline: A take-charge approach for today's educator*. Canter and Associates: Los Angeles.

Cowen, EL, Pedro-Carroll, JL & Alpert-Gillis, LJ (1990) 'Relationships between support and adjustment among children of divorce'. *Journal of Child Psychology and Psychiatry and Allied Disciplines*, *31*, 727–35.

Cullen, M & Wilks, R (1983) 'Fly me to the moon: A classroom behaviour management program to enhance learning'. *InterView*, *10*, 27–31.

DeLucia-Waack, JL & Gerrity, D (2001) 'Effective groupwork for elementary school-age children whose parents are divorcing'. *Family Journal Counseling and Therapy for Couples and Families*, *9*, 273–84.

Dodge, KA (1993) 'The future of research on the treatment of conduct disorder'. *Development and Psychopathology*, *5*, 311–19.

Elson-Green, J (2002) 'Review could help elevate the teaching profession'. *Campus Review, 5 (9)*, 7–9.

Emmer, E, Evertson, C & Anderson, L (1980) 'Effective classroom management at the beginning of the school year'. *Elementary School Journal, 80*, 219–31.

Fergusson, DM, Horwood, LJ & Lynskey, M (1994) 'The childhoods of multiple problem adolescents: A fifteen year longitudinal study'. *Journal of Child Psychology and Psychiatry, 35*, 1123–40.

Freiberg, JH (1983) 'Consistency: The key to classroom management'. *Journal of Education for Teaching, 9*, 1–15.

Fuller, A (1998) *From surviving to thriving: promoting mental health in young people.* ACER Press: Melbourne.

Galloway, D, Rogers, C, Armstrong, D & Leo, E (1998) *Motivating the difficult to teach.* Longman: London.

Giallo, R & Little, E (2003) 'Classroom behaviour problems: The relationship between preparedness, classroom experiences, and self-efficacy in graduate and student teachers'. *Australian Journal of Educational and Developmental Psychology, 3*, 21–34.

Gladding, ST (1991) *Group work: A counselling specialty.* Merrill: New York.

Good, TL & Brophy, JE (1994) *Looking into classrooms* (6th ed). Harper & Row: New York.

Gordon, C, Arthur, M & Butterfield, N (1996) *Promoting positive behaviour: An Australian guide to classroom management.* Thomas Nelson: Melbourne.

Guldner, CA & O'Connor, T (1991) 'The ALF group: A model of group therapy with children'. *Journal of Group psychotherapy, Psychodrama, & Sociometry, 43*, 184–90.

Hetherington, EM, Bridges, M & Insabella, GM (1998) 'What matters? What does not? Five perspectives on the association between marital transitions and children's adjustment'. *American Psychologist, 53*, 167–84.

Hodges, WF (1986) *Interventions for children of divorce.* John Wiley & Sons: New York.

References

Infantino, J & Little, E (2003) 'Students' perceptions of classroom behaviour problems and the effectiveness of disciplinary methods'. *Paper submitted for publication.*

Kazdin, AE (1995) *Conduct disorders in childhood and adolescence* (2nd ed). Sage: Thousand Oaks, CA.

Kos, JM, Richdale, AR & Jackson, MS (2002) 'Knowledge about Attention-Deficit/ Hyperactivity Disorder: A comparison of in-service and pre-service teachers'. *Paper submitted for publication.*

Kounin, JS (1970) *Discipline and group management in classrooms.* Peter H. Wyden: NY.

Little, E (1999) 'Conduct disorder: generalisation across settings and implications for home and school based interventions'. *Unpublished doctoral thesis, RMIT University.*

Little, E (2001) 'Secondary school teachers perceptions of classroom behaviour problems'. *Paper submitted for publication.*

Little, E, Hudson, A & Wilks, R (2000) 'Conduct problems across home and school'. *Behaviour Change, 17*, 1–9.

Little, E, Hudson, A & Wilks, R (2002) 'The efficacy of written teacher advice (tip sheets) for managing classroom behaviour problems'. *Educational Psychology, 22*, 251–66.

Lochman, JE, Lampron, LB, Gemmer, TV & Harris, R (1987) 'Anger coping intervention with aggressive children: A guide to implementation in school settings'. In PA Keller & SR Heyman (Eds), *Innovations in clinical practice: A source book (Vol. 6).* (pp. 339–56). Professional Resource Exchange: Sarasota, FL.

Loeber, R (1990) 'Development and risk factors of juvenile antisocial behaviour and delinquency'. *Clinical Psychology Review, 10*, 1–41.

McGrath, H & Francey, S (1991) *Friendly kids, friendly classrooms: teaching social skills and confidence in the classroom.* Longman Cheshire: Melbourne.

Merrett, FE & Wheldall, K (1993) 'How do teachers learn to manage classroom behaviour? A study of teachers opinions about their initial training with special reference to classroom behavior management'. *Educational Studies, 19*, 91–105.

Miller, A (1995) 'Teachers' attributions of causality, control and responsibility in respect of difficult pupil behaviour and its successful management'. *Educational Psychology, 15,* 457–71.

Nansel, TR, Overpeck, M, Pilla, RS, Ruan, WJ, Simons-Morton, B & Scheidt, P (2001) 'Bullying behaviors among US youth: prevalence and association with psychological adjustment'. *Journal of the American Medical Association, 285,* 2094–100.

National Health and Medical Research Council (1997) *Attention deficit hyperactivity disorder.* Author: Canberra.

Pedro-Carroll, JL & Cowen, EL (1985) 'The Children of Divorce Intervention Program: An investigation of the efficacy of a school based prevention program'. *Journal of Consulting and Clinical Psychology, 53,* 603–11.

Pedro-Carroll, JL, Sutton, SE & Wyman, PA (1999) 'A two-year follow-up evaluation of a preventive intervention for young children of divorce'. *School Psychology Review, 28,* 467–76.

Pullis, M (1991) 'Practical considerations of excluding conduct disordered students: An empirical analysis'. *Behavioral Disorders, 17,* 9–22.

Richardson, CD & Rosen, LA (1999) 'School based interventions for children of divorce'. *Professional School Counseling, 3,* 21–6.

Rigby, K (1996) *Bullying in schools and what to do about it.* ACER: Melbourne.

Sainbury, M, Whetton, C, Mason, K & Schagen, I (1998) 'Fallback in attainment on transfer at age 11. Evidence from the summer literacy schools evaluation'. *Educational Research, 40,* 73–81.

Sanders, MR & Dadds, MR (1993) *Behavioral Family Intervention.* Allyn and Bacon: Needham Heights, MA.

Semrud-Clikeman, M, Biederman, J, Sprich-Buckminster, S, Lehman, BK, Faraone, SV & Norman, D (1992) *Journal of the American Academy of Child and Adolescent Psychiatry, 31,* 439–48.

Shifflett, K & Cummings, EM (1999) 'A program for educating parents about the effects of divorce and conflict on children: An initial evaluation'. *Family Relations: Interdisciplinary Journal of Applied Family Studies, 48*, 79–89.

Short, RJ & Shapiro, SK (1993) 'Conduct disorders: A framework for understanding and intervention in schools and communities'. *School Psychology Review, 22*, 362–75.

Stolberg, AL & Mahler, J (1994) 'Enhancing treatment gains in a school-based intervention for children of divorce through skill training, parental involvement, and transfer procedures'. *Journal of Consulting and Clinical Psychology, 62*, 147–56.

Sutherland, KS (2000) 'Promoting positive interactions between teachers and students with emotional/behavioural disorders'. *Preventing School Failure, 44*, 110–14.

Tingstrom, DH & Edwards, R (1989) 'Eliminating common misconceptions about behavioural psychology: One step toward increased academic productivity'. *Psychology in the Schools, 26*, 194–202.

Wheldall, K & Merrett, FE (1988) 'Which behaviours do primary school teachers say they find most troublesome?' *Educational Review, 40*, 13–27.

Wilson, J & Wing Jan, L (1995) 'Developing reflective learning to improve classroom management'. *Reflect*, 1(2), 6–12.

Wolfgang, CH & Glickman, CD (1980) *Solving discipline problems: Strategies for classroom teachers.* Allyn and Bacon, Inc: Boston, MS.

Woolfolk, A (1993) *Educational Psychology* (5th ed.), Allyn & Bacon: NY.

Appendix—Prize vouchers, token and certificate

THIS VOUCHER ENTITLES YOU TO

Choose a book from the special box

THIS VOUCHER ENTITLES YOU TO

A lucky dip on Friday

REFERENCES

117

STAR STUDENT!

_____

FOR

_____